Frederick Thomas Hodgson

The hardwood finisher : with rules and directions

Frederick Thomas Hodgson

The hardwood finisher : with rules and directions

ISBN/EAN: 9783337157050

Printed in Europe, USA, Canada, Australia, Japan

Cover: Foto ©Andreas Hilbeck / pixelio.de

More available books at **www.hansebooks.com**

THE

HARDWOOD FINISHER.

WITH RULES AND DIRECTIONS,

FOR FINISHING IN NATURAL COLORS AND IN ANTIQUE,
MAHOGANY, CHERRY, BIRCH, WALNUT, OAK, ASH, RED-
WOOD, SYCAMORE, PINE, AND ALL OTHER DOMES-
TIC WOODS.

FINISHING, FILLING, STAINING, VARNISHING, AND POLISHING.

ALSO:
MISCELLANEOUS RULES FOR DYEING, GILDING, AND BRONZING

COMPILED AND EDITED BY
F R E D T. H O D G S O N,
Editor of THE OPERATIVE BUILDER.
Late Editor of "BUILDER AND WOOD-WORKER," and "CABINET-MAKER
AND UPHOLSTERER."

NEW YORK:
THE INDUSTRIAL PUBLICATION COMPANY,

PREFACE.

THE subject of wood-finishing is one that interests every person who has anything to do with the construction or decoration of buildings, be he architect, carpenter and joiner, painter, decorator or carver, and it is to meet the requirements of these artists and artisans, in these respects, that this work has been prepared.

In order to make the book as complete as possible it has been necessary to consult a variety of authorities on the subject, and cull from them whatever in my opinion—based on experience—I thought best, and here and there add to, or eliminate, such matter as my experience proved to be good on the one hand, and what I thought useless or absurd on the other.

I am of course aware that there are some methods of finishing that I have not touched upon; such as the finishing of musical instruments, toys, wooden bric-a-brac, laquered Japanned ware, walking sticks, etc., etc., but as this work is only intended for the finishing of wood-work employed in the construction and completion of buildings, it was thought better to confine it to that department alone; thereby keeping its cost within reasonable limits.

Among the works drawn from I may mention, CABINET-MAKING AND UPHOLSTERY, THE BUILDER AND WOOD-WORKERS, CARPENTRY AND BUILDING, SCIENTIFIC AMERICAN, FURNITURE MEN'S MANUAL, SPON'S WORKSHOP RECEIPTS, THE WORKSHOP COMPANION, ENGLISH MECHANIC, HOUSE PAINTING AND DECORATING, THE PAINTERS MAGAZINE AND COACH PAINTER, ENCYCLOPEDIA BRITANNICA, ninth edition, and many other works.

While believing the work, as now presented to be equal, if not superior to any published on the subject ; I feel that it is defective in some minor points ; as it would be impossible to convey to the mind of the operator all the minutæ of each and every process required in wood-finishing ; for the perfect wood-finisher can only be the outcome of experience and observation added to the knowledge and instructions derived from the teachings of others. The latter is offered in this volume ; the experience and observation must rest with the learner ; and if he takes advantage of his opportunities and masters all the details offered herewith, there is no valid reason why he should not become an expert WOOD-FINISHER.

FRED T. HODGSON.

NEW YORK,
August, 1892.

INTRODUCTION.

DOUBTLESS, the arts of Carpentry and Joinery were among the oldest in the world, and these arts must have flourished for many centuries before anything like polish or fine finish on wood-work were even thought of. The handles of stone weapons were probably the first specimens of the wood-worker's art, then clubs and other wooden weapons subsequently the "dug-out" and the paddle or oar. Huts or wooden dwellings with doors and shutters, roofs and floors did not appear until much later.

Nature always makes her works fittest for the intended end, and beautiful as well. So long as mankind were in constant contact with Nature's works they tried to imitate her methods, but at last this involved two processes, so, that, when they ceased to care for beauty, they grudged the necessary labor required to attain it. Therefore, in anything made by the hands of man, with no other motive in view but that of utility, the chances are a thousand to one that beauty will be conspicuous only by its absence.

That wood plays a very important part in the affairs of mankind, I scarcely need mention, and nature seems to have well understood our wants for it is claimed by those who claim to know, that about one-third of the earth's surface is covered with trees, all of which are capable of contributing in some form or another to the wants of man.

In this country, the art of using wood for almost every purpose, has gone far beyond anything that has ever been attempted by any other people. The introduction of wood-working machinery for the rapid manipulation of intricate mouldings,

(5)

spirals, flutings, beadings and carvings, has in a great measure,
had a tendency to elevate the taste of the whole community,
though I must confess that artistic excellence of a high order, in
the mechanical arts, is now scarcely found among our younger
workmen ; machinery having almost done away with the necessity for the fine kinds of hand and brain work.   Fashion, which
rules despotically in the wardrobe, influences, to a greater or
lesser degree, the style and finish of wood-work, and to a certain
extent, the kind of wood that must be used for certain purposes.
It is but a few years since, when no other wood than clean white
pine, would be permitted to do service in a building.   Every
thing must be pine, floors, doors, windows, and skirtings, even
to the bath fittings.   Then Dame fashion sent forth her decree,
and a mixture of white pine, Norway and Southern pine, was
used followed shortly afterward by the abominable mixture of ash,
walnut and chestnut.   Some architect who desereves well of his
country, introduced all walnut and all mahogany fitments ; and
at once, people of taste who saw this manner of finish noticed its
superiority over the "trash-like" mixture at once ; and the
fashion then of finishing in one kind of wood became the rage.
Walnut was found too dark for general purposes and was soon
abandoned for the lighter woods ; chestnut, sycamore, ash and
oak were then tried, but I believe I voice the opinion of a majority of architects when I say that, with the exception of oak, the
light colored woods were not successful, from an æsthetic point of
view, and it is on record, that many buildings finished in these
woods, have recently had their wood-work cleaned and stained
to imitate darker woods or have been painted.   One of the valuable qualities of white oak, is, that it grows richer in color as it
gets older, and no matter how it is finished, so long as the grain
is visible, it mellows and improves with age.   This is a quality
that no other of our American woods possess in the same degree.
All the oaks have this quality to a certain extent, but the white
oak (Quercus alba), possesses it more than any other.   Mahogany
too, has this quality largely, if true Spanish mahogany is used,

but little of this is in the market ; though there are many woods which have the appearance of mahogany, and are called mahogany, and both buyer and user are oftentimes deceived, and pay for what they do not get.

We have often been reproached with willfully or ignorantly ignoring or destroying our own handsome woods, while importing from abroad at excessive cost, and the payment of heavy duties, foreign woods which are much inferior to many of our native productions. This folly prevailed at a time when it was fashionable and even popular to believe there was no merit in domestic productions of any sort, this state of things, however is now at an end ; and in the neighborhood of all large towns, and in country places as well ; a finish in hard wood is the rule, and a finish in pine the exception, if the building to be finished, makes any pretension of being "up to the times."

With regard to the difference in cost between a finish in the best clear pine, and the best selected hard wood, there is really but little, if any, if we take into consideration durability and good taste. As between pine wood and good well finished hard wood, the disparity in value and merit is so very little as to completely silence any comparison. Between poor pine and poor hard wood the preference should by all means be given to the former ; because, poor pine as it reveals its defects can be puttied and painted in a manner to disguise them ; whereas the defects of poor hard wood are almost incurable. The rationale of the subject seems to resolve itself into the following statement.

Modern taste in expensive dwellings calls for the free use of hard woods. It is immaterial which are used, but highly essential that the best seasoned woods should be selected ; and, further, that they should be skillfully treated and finished.

The principal recommendation of hard wood is that it admits of a treatment which renders it impervious to the effects of atmospheric changes, and, therefore can be made more durable and ultimately less expensive than pine wood. A hard wood that is well seasoned before use, that is treated with proper fillers to close up its pores, and then finished with successive coats of copal varnish, well rubbed in with pumice stone, being finally brought to a higher flat finish, presents the most attractive, serviceable and reliable style of wood-work that can be introduced into a house. Well finished hard wood obviates the expense and annoyance of constant renewals, which pine work calls for in patching, puttying and painting. The most brilliant gloss of finished hard wood can be restored by a skilled person without disturbing the furniture or carpets of a house.

Pine work seems peculiarly and incomparably adapted for cheap work. A good article of common pine, suitable for ordinary work can be procured, and worked at considerably less expense than would be involved in using good hard wood. The use of poor hard wood in any work should not be tolerated or thought of under any circumstances, for the simple reason that it is certain to create annoyance and expense, which no house-owner, especially of moderate priced property, should be subjected to.

I have deemed the foregoing introduction necessary as it will enable the workman to have some idea of the development of the art of joinery, and the transition from the use of pine and the softer woods, to that of the hard woods.

In the following work it is my intention to take each of the woods most in use ; describe them, say what I think they are best adapted for, and the best way to finish them, as far as my knowledge extends. By this means the reader will have, under one head, all the book contains concerning the particular wood he is about to finish.

PRELIMINARY.

If the workman who finally finishes wood-work, had the selection of the materials out of which the work is formed ; and wrought the work himself ; the following suggestions would scarcely be required, for he would see to it that the material was free from shakes, cracks, worm holes, doze, sap and fractures ; and he would so choose his material, that the full beauty of the grain would show, when the polish coat went on. He would also see, that the work was *clean*. That is, that no plane marks were visible, no rough spots, or cross-grains noticeable, and that all angles were sharp and definite, all mouldings smooth and not a nail head or screw top to be seen, nor any point that could suggest a nail head. As a rule, however, the workman who puts on the last finishing touches never makes the work, though he is *always* expected to cover and hide all the faults of bad workmanship, bad selection of timber, and a thousand other objectionable things in connection with work, over which he has had no control. In order to aid the finisher as much as possible, I give a few hints herewith, for the use of the workman whose duty it may be to prepare and put up the work to be finished. The suggestions given, are equally applicable for hard and soft woods and I trust they will not be out of place.

First, then see that the material is dry, free from imperfections, of the full sizes required, and of such variety of grain as may be suitable for the purpose intended. Next, make all joints close and as near perfect as possible as on this point rests, in a great measure, the artistic appearance of the work. Make all angles sharp and clean, and all mitered mouldings true and with perfect intersections. Never use glass paper where a scraper can be ap-

(9)

plied, and when a large quantity of mouldings of similar contour and size are to be employed ; it is always better to make a scraper their reverse shape, and use it in cleaning and preparing the mouldings for the varnisher, than to use glass paper for the purpose.

Wherever possible and suitable I would advise the use of glue in putting up finish, and I may here remark to the workman, that after a little practice in the use of glue and a little knowledge of its worth and capabilities, he will prefer it, to nails or screws where he can apply it ; further on I will give a few hints and suggestions on the proper methods of using glue in house finishing. Of course, I am well aware that the use of nails and screws is a necessity in wood finishing, but where the work is to be left natural color, or stained and polished, there should not be the slightest suspicion of a nail or screw head, and to meet this condition the skilled workman resorts to several expedients to hide the fastenings among which are the following.   These methods, which are similar, are called '' sliver-nailing,'' or sometimes, '' chip blind-nailing.''   In the first method, shown at Fig. 1, the

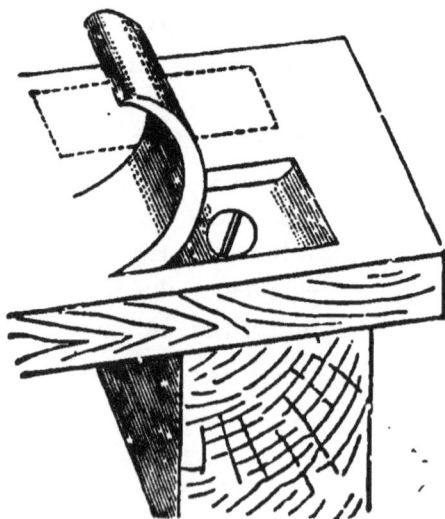

Fig. 1.

wood is raised with a firmer chisel and the screw or nail is then put in place and driven home.   At Fig. 2, the "sliver" or chip,

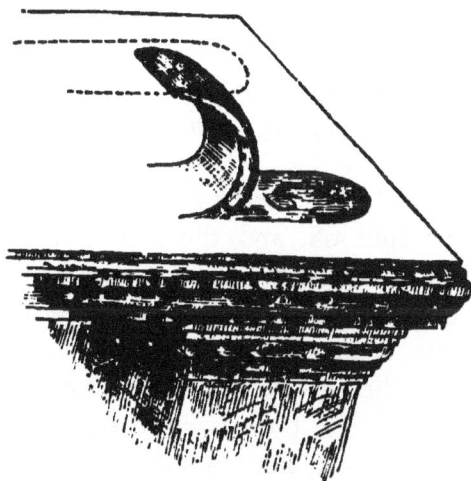

Fig. 2.

is raised with a gouge.   In the first instance a sharp knife should be employed to draw lengthwise with the grain two deep cuts the width of the chisel, as this keeps the sides of the chip from splitting.   The chisel should be set at a steep angle at first till the proper depth is reached, and then made to turn out a cut of even thickness until there is room to drive in a screw or nail.   If too sharp a curve is given, the "sliver" is likely to break apart in being straightened out again.   In Fig. 2, I show how the "sliver" is raised by using a gouge.   To do this nicely a gouge about three-quarters of an inch across the face should be used and the curve should be quick.   In this case no knife cut is needed, as the corners of the gouge will cut as it progresses.

The cut being made and the "sliver" slightly raised as shown in both cuts, the screw or nail may be driven without disturbing either the "sliver" or the cut underneath.   See that the head of either screw or nail be sunk beneath surface of recess, so that the "sliver" will fit back in its place without obstruction.   Now take properly prepared glue and, after warming the "sliver" and recess with a warm cloth, cover the underside of "sliver" and the wood underneath, seeing that the glue is not too thick; press down the "sliver" in place, then rub with the face of a hammer until the glue holds; then leave until dry, when the whole may be dressed off and finished. Another way is to glue the "sliver" down and then take a flat piece of pine about an inch thick, and glue over the "sliver," rubbing the pine block to and fro until the glue takes. The block is left on until dry and solid. The pine block may be split off, and the face of the wood dressed clean and finished. . In hard-wood finish for interior housework this latter plan of fastening up stuff is often resorted to.

When the work has been made secure by any or all the methods described, the next thing to be considered is the smoothing and final finishing, and these two processes as here defined, pertain to all sorts of wood, hard or soft, that is intended to be finished in the natural colors or stained. In order to obtain a fine and substantial finish the work must either be smoothed fine with a plane, scraped with a steel scraper, or rubbed down with the finest glass paper. For very hard or irregular grained wood, such as is made into veneers or employed for the finer kinds of work, the cleaning-off process consists first in planing the surfaces with a toothed plane, having a serrated edge like a comb, this tool scratching away the high places and leveling the surface without pulling or splintering the wood, as a common knife will do unless very carefully adjusted and worked. After tooth-planing, the surfaces are scraped with a steel hand scraper until the scratches made by a tooth plane are removed, and the surface is then finished by rubbing with glass-paper of different finenesses.

Straight-grained hard woods can be cleaned off by planing with a common smoothing plane, and then scraping and rubbing them with glass-paper. Soft wood requires only careful planing and glass-papering, but if scraping is omitted great care must be taken in planing, or else the plane marks will show by reflection when the surface is polished, varnished or painted. I have known of cases where the finishers were wrongly accused of improper execution of the work because the finish, after being exposed to the changes of temperature occurring in a year, became impaired on account of the appearance of fine cracks running with the grain, differing from those caused by the improper application of varnish, which always runs across the grain. Among other reasons for this premature impairment, one is that the fine fibres become affected; sandpapering the wood lengthwise or with the grain will loosen these, but will not break them off. The application of the filler will force them down into the pores, the filler making them adhere perfectly tight for some time; but the changing of the temperature expands and contracts the wood, thus causing the fibres to loosen and work out, making their appearance in fine cracks and impairing the finish.

This fault most frequently occurs in open-grained wood especially when employed in the common class of cabinet-work which is transferred to the finishing-room directly upon leaving the machinery where it has been sandpapered lengthwise by a set of cylinders under heavy pressure, and should be guarded against with great care. "This sandpapering," finishers will generally say, "is a matter for the cabinet maker or the carpenter; daub it over and let it go." It is immaterial to them how the finish holds out after leaving their hands; but I find it is well for a finisher to do his duty by at least insisting upon having the work lightly cross-sandpapered with paper with No. 1. or No. 1½ paper. This process will loosen the fibres at both ends; consequently, they will fall off, or, if they do not do so, they should be dusted off previous to filling.

There is one more source of injury which should be guarded against with great care, and that is finishing over wet timber; nor should steam, water or dampness in any form be allowed to come in contact with the smooth dry surface, as it will raise the grain, making redressing by the joiner a necessity.

In their natural state all woods are more or less porous consisting of bundles of hard fibres, with interstices filled with a softer substance. These constitute the grain, and as the hard or soft parts predominate, the wood is said to be hard, fine, or close-grained, or soft and open-grained. To fill these softer parts, or pores, and give to the whole an even, uniform surface, hard, and capable of a brilliant polish, is the object of the finishers' art. This hard, firm surface was formerly gained by the successive application of several coats of varnish, at least three preliminary coats being required to fill the pores; the inequalities were then reduced by fine sand or glass-paper, and several additional coats laid on, the last, after becoming thoroughly hard being polished if desired. In this operation, however, a great quantity of varnish is absorbed by the open pores of the wood, and it is consequently so expensive that it is now seldom used. Recourse is therefore had to various plans to render the wood non-absorbent before applying varnishes, and certain compounds called fillers are largely used for this purpose. These I will endeavor to describe, and give the methods of application in the following section.

WOOD-FILLERS AND WOOD-FILLING.

In woods employed for house and cabinet work there are two distinct natures, therefore different treatment is required in finishing. First, there is the coarse or open-grained wood, having its surface perforated with innumerable pores or cells. In order to obtain a smooth and even finish, these pores should be filled up to a level with the hard grain, or, as the grainer would term them, the "lights" of the wood. Next we have the fine or close-grained wood, which, like the preceding, also contains these pores, but they are of a very fine character, and simply sealing them up with a liquid filler will enable one to produce a fine smooth finish, which we shall consider farther on.

I will now return to the open or wide-grained wood which requires more attention and care than the closer-grained wood, if same results are expected. There are many things that will serve the purpose of fillers and make pretty fair work; among these may be mentioned, china clay, silver white and corn starch ; the best of which is probably the last named. This is well adapted to the work being equally useful with light, or when colored with dark wood ; one fault with it, is that it never hardens. China clay— the English is the best—makes an exceedingly good filler; it is light in color, very fine and dries as hard as cement.

There are an hundred ways of preparing fillers for use, and nearly as many different materials for making them ; I would recommend however, that wherever it is possible, that Wheeler's patent quartz filler be used; though I am aware, that in many cases, it may not be advisable to use it, and to meet these rare conditions the following mixtures may be substituted.

A filler should be so mixed that the greater portion of the vehicle will penetrate into the wood, leaving the pigment on the surface to be rubbed into the pores and still retain enough combining property to form a hard and impenetrable surface. This depends entirely upon the proportions of the vehicles employed, and, as different pigments require different quantities of vehicle, I seldom mix filler by actual measurement unless it be in large amounts. I proceed with the mixing by filling my pot two-thirds full of the dry pigment, then add boiled linseed oil, producing the consistency of putty, then dilute with about one part japan and two parts turpentine. Should it be required to keep the wood as light as possible, replace the boiled oil with raw, using a smaller quantity, but a little more japan. For all light wood the light japan should be preferred, although there are many who never use anything but the common brown. Naptha can also be employed in place of the turpentine, somewhat reducing the expense ; but, as naptha evaporates much faster, it prevents the operator from covering an extended surface without running the risk of having it dry hard. This causes difficulty at "rubbing it in" and wiping off the surplus, although "wiping off" should not proceed until the filler has flatted—or, at least, "set." This to a certain extent the operator can accelerate or retard by omitting or adding a small quantity of oil, keeping in view the fact that the smaller the quantity of oil used, the lighter colored, but the less durable, will be the finish.

Oil is sometimes used as a filler, but its use is not recommended; applied directly to the wood, its effect is to swell the fibres, or "raise the grain," which remains in that condition until the oil becomes entirely dry or disappears. During this time the fibres are gradually shrinking, and consequently moving or checking the varnish. The qualities essential to a good filler are that it shall readily enter the porous portion of the wood, and shall very soon harden and render the wood impervious to the varnish, which should lie smoothly upon the surface, giving brilliancy and effect to the natural beauty of the wood; and that it shall not raise the grain of the wood; and that it shall not change the color of the wood. These conditions are satisfactorily fulfilled by few of the home-made fillers ordinarily used in shops, and while I give a number of receipts, my readers are advised that they will obtain better satisfaction, at less cost by purchasing some of the patent fillers now coming into general use. In these fillers very little oil is used and a large amount of dryers, so that the wood becomes perfectly dry and hard in a few hours preventing any swelling or shrinking of the fibres of the wood after the varnish is applied. The following fillers should be allowed to dry until quite hard. A period of about eight hours is usually sufficient, but it is better to let the work stand for twenty-four hours before touching it with glass-paper. In applying a filler it should always be borne in mind that the substance of wood consists of a multitude of small tubes lying side by side. These tubes or cells are not continuous from top to bottom of the tree, but are comparatively short and taper out to points so that they are thickest in the middle. Most of the common woods have the walls of these tubes so thin that liquid is readily absorbed by them and carried into the substance for some distance. Different kinds of wood differ much in the shape and arrangement of these cells. In filling the pores the first step is taken in providing an absolutely smooth surface. We trust mainly to mechanical force in rubbing in, aided by the absorptive powers of the wood. Formerly successive varnishings and rubbings and scrapings took much time and when they were done, the final finish had still to be applied, but the whole process has now been simplified, by using fillers. The careful workman will not leave "great daubs" of superfluous filler here and there on the work, but will see that all corners and heads and quirks of mouldings are well cleaned off before it gets too hard to remove easily, and should there be any nail holes—which there ought not to be—he will have them filled with properly colored putty or cement and nicely smoothed down before he makes any attempt to put on his finishing coats.

Among the many homemade fillers I have endeavored to select the best.

Walnut Filler.—For Medium and Cheap Work.—10 lbs. bolted English whiting, 3 lbs. dry burnt umber, 4 lbs. Vandyke brown, 3 lbs. calcined plaster, ½ lb. Venetian red, 1 gal. boiled linseed oil, ½ gal. spirits turpentine, 1 quart black japan. Mix well and apply with brush; rub well with excelsior or tow, clean off with rags.

Walnut Filler.—For Imitation Wax-Finish.—5 lbs. bolted whiting, 1 lb. calcined plaster, 6 oz. calcined magnesia, 1 oz. dry burnt umber, 1 oz. French yellow, 1 quart raw linseed oil, 1 quart benzine spirits, ½ pint very thin white shellac. Mix well and apply with a brush. Rub well in and clean off with rags. Before using the above filling give the work one coat of white shellac. When dry, sand-paper down and apply the filler.

Walnut Filler.—For First-Class Work.—3 lbs. burnt umber, ground in oil, 1 lb. burnt sienna, ground in oil, 1 quart spirits of turpentine, 1 pint brown japan. Mix well and apply with a brush; sand-paper well; clean off with tow and rags. This gives a beautiful chocolate color to the wood.

Filler for Light Woods.—5 lbs. bolted English whiting, 3 lbs. calcined plaster, 1 lb. corn starch, 3 oz. calcined magnesia, ½ gallon raw linseed oil, 1 quart spirits of turpentine, 1 quart brown

2

japan, and sufficient French yellow to tinge the white. Mix well and apply with a brush, rub in with excelsior or tow, and clean off with rags.

Filler for Cherr·.—5 lbs. bolted English whiting, 2 lbs. calcined plaster, 1½ oz. dry burnt sienna, 1 oz. Venetian red, 1 quart boiled linseed oil, 1 pint spirits of turpentine, 1 pint brown japan. Mix well, rub in with excelsior or tow and clean off with rags.

Filler for Oak.—5 lbs. bolted English whiting, 2 lbs. calcined plaster, 1 oz. dry burnt sienna, ½ oz. dry French yellow, 1 quart raw linseed oil, 1 pint benzine spirits, ½ pint white shellac. Mix well, apply with brush, rub in with excelsior or tow, and clean off with rags.

Filler for Rosewood.—6 lbs. bolted English whiting, 2 lbs. calcined plaster, 1 lb. rose pink, 2 oz. Venetian red, ½ lb. Vandyke brown, ½ lb. brandon red, 1 gallon boiled linseed oil, ½ gallon spirits of turpentine, 1 quart black japan. Mix well, apply with brush, rub in with excelsior or tow, and clean off with rags.

Another.—Stir boiled oil and corn-starch into a very thick paste ; add a little japan, and reduce with turpentine, but add no color for light ash. For dark ash and chestnut use a little raw sienna ; for walnut, burnt umber, add a small quantity of Venetian red ; for bay wood, burnt sienna. In no case use more color than is required to overcome the white appearance of the starch, unless it is wished to stain the wood. The filler is worked with brush and rags in the usual manner. Let it dry forty-eight hours, or until it is in condition to rub down with No. o sandpaper without much gumming up, and if an extra fine finish is desired, fill again with the same materials, using less oil, but more of japan and turpentine.

Another.—Take three papers corn-starch, one quart boiled linseed oil, two quarts turpentine, one-quarter pint japan ; cut in half the turpentine before mixing ; it will not cut perfectly otherwise. For dark woods add burnt umber to color. When nearly dry rub off with cloths. The above mixture must be used fresh, as it is of no value after it is four or five days old. The cloths used in rubbing as above mentioned should be destroyed immediately after use, as spontaneous combustion is likely to ensue from the ingredients employed.

Preparation of Wood for Staining.—As a filler of wood to be stained, apply French plaster of Paris, mixed as a creamy paste with water, and after rubbing in, clean any surplus off; or use whiting finely powdered, or white lead slacked with painters' drying oil, and used as a filler. Another process is that of oiling, then rubbing crosswise to the grain with a sponge dipped in thin polish composed of melted beeswax, resin, and shellac, and smoothing the surface, when dry, with pumice-stone, or fine glass paper. Embody the work a second time with thicker polish, cr a mixture of polish and varnish. The rubbers will work easily with half the quantity of oil which is ordinarily used. This second body should be rubbed very smooth with moist putty.

In the use of any filler, care must be taken in the selection of color, for the employment of a light colored filler on dark wood or *vice versa* would result in gross defacement, as the lighter color would show at the pores of the wood in the one case, and the darker in the other. Therefore, to avoid this the filler should be as near as possible the color of the wood to be filled.

As a general thing, paint manufacturers who do not make fillers a specialty use opaque colors to stain their filler, as it requires a less quantity. This will do sometimes, but not always. But those which give to the wood a clear and bright appearance, and therefore produce the best results, are stained with transparent colors; those chiefly employed are burnt umber and sienna, Venetian red, Vandyke brown and charcoal black, the charcoal being ground fine in oil, while the others can be used dry and according to the following recipes with good results :

In mixing any or all dark fillers the same pigments used for the light (previously described) should be kept for a basis, with sufficient coloring to stain it to the desired depth of shade.

Filler for Walnut is very often stained with burnt umber ; this is reddish in hue and gives to the wood a pleasing effect. Others use Venetian red darkened somewhat with lamp black; this is rather opaque, and tends to deaden the color of the wood. There is another article—namely, Vandyke brown—which gives fair results. In order to obtain a rich effect, the filler should be made considerably darker than the wood when new.

Fillers for mahogany, cherry, California redwood, and other woods of similar shade, should be stained with burnt sienna, as they should be finished very clear. It is well to know that charcoal black, and Venetian red will give the desired shade for any dark-colored wood in common use or for all colors in antique, but it does not show up quite as clear as some other combinations.

For rosewood, charcoal as a stain will suffice, and for vanilla or Brazil-wood the use of rose-pink will give good results.

The methods of mixing these fillers are quite numerous. It is impossible to give the proportions definitely, owing to the strength of the colors or the transparency of the chief ingredient, but one cannot go astray by following the preceding rules.

Mix the light pigment to a paste with boiled oil, which must be well stirred up. Then in another pot mix a quantity of the colored pigment with turpentine or naphtha; and when thoroughly "cut," or dissolved, add sufficient of it to the light to give the shade required. After this is obtained, dilute with turpentine or naphtha and japan, as directed in mixing light filler. This applies to all colors except black, which is seldom obtained finely ground unless in oil, and properly thinned down.

There are many finishers and firms who exclusively use manufactured fillers, and in consequence meet with many difficulties as to the shade they require, as different manufacturers use different colors to stain their filler. But this difficulty can be overcome by a few experiments with the above-named stains.

As the foregoing gives pretty nearly all the fillers in general use with the exception of some of the manufactured mineral preparations of which I will have more to say further on, I will now proceed to describe the method of application, and for the greater portion of this description, and other matters in this work, I am indebted to Mr. R. A. A. Bahre's papers on the subject contributed to *House-Painting and Decorating*, a monthly magazine published in the city of New York.

The secret of this is to do the work well, quickly and economically. These points are dealt with in the following:

Have your filler mixed to the consistency of ordinary lead paint; then apply to the prepared surface of the wood with a pound brush, or, what is still better, a 3-0 or 4-0 oval chisel varnish brush. In applying the filler it is not necessary to cover all the small beads and carvings; and if the filler be light better avoid coating them at all, and if dark or antique stain them with a little of the filler, much reduced with spirits of turpentine. For this purpose have at hand a small pot with a small fitch or sash tool.

By not filling the beads and carvings, the varnish is not so liable to run down in them, although sufficient remains to produce a finish equal to the balance of the surface.

After enough surface has been covered with the filler, so that what has been first applied begins to flatten, the process of wiping should immediately begin, using for that purpose either a rag or a handful of waste or Excelsior. If the wood is very open grained, waste is preferable. With a piece of this that has previously been used and is pretty well supplied with filler, rub crosswise of the grain, rather rubbing it into the grain than wiping it off. After the whole surface has been gone over in this way, take a clean piece of waste or rag (never use Excelsior for wiping clean) and wipe the surface perfectly clean and free from filler, using a wooden pick the point of which has been covered with a rag or waste to clean out the corners, beads, etc. It is well to give these picks some attention, as a person once accustomed to certain tools can accomplish more and better work than with tools that feel strange in his hands; therefore, each finisher should furnish his own pick. As to their construction, these are best made from second-growth hickory, which can be procured at any carriage repair shop, such as old spokes, broken felloes, etc. They are made eight inches in length, half inch oval at one end and tapering down to the point at the other. Sharpen the oval end like a cold chisel, then smooth with sandpaper, which should also be used to sharpen the tool when the same becomes worn dull.

This picking out of the filler from beads, etc., can be accelerated by the use of a picking brush manufactured especially for that purpose, but it is not advisable to use this on very coarsely grained wood, as it scrubs the filler out of the pores.

There are several fillers used which do not require this picking and scrubing. One is a liquid filler used chiefly for carriage finishing ; but it can be used successfully on butternut, bird's-eye maple, curly maple, satinwood, hickory, etc. It is made from gum and oil. Another is a filler made from finely-ground pumice stone, mixed as other fillers. It is applied with a brush, and must be left to dry at least twenty-four hours; it is then sandpapered smooth, when an oil varnish is applied, rendering it completely transparent. This last can be used only upon light wood.

The workman, as a matter of course, will understand that different woods, require slightly different treatment, and the finer-grained woods, among which are the pines, maples, cedars and poplars, of different varieties, and birch, cherry, beech, sycamore, white box, satinwood, etc., require no filling, not that a filling would prove detrimental to the finish—except upon stained work or white holly, which in order to maintain a clear color should never be filled—but, from the condition of all fine wood, it is superfluous, and only causes unnecessary labor and expense. At this point it will be convenient to pause to consider the subject of mineral or prepared wood-fillers.

I think I have prepared the mind of the reader to receive the fact, that of all the several manufactured preparations in the market I think that Wheeler's patent filler made by the Bridgeport Wood-Finishing Company, is decidedly the best and the most

economical to use, for many reasons, the chief one being its certainty of action. A great deal of time and money have been
wasted in attempting to make good fillers, to no purpose, and a
great variety, as I have shown—of substances as chalk, plaster of
Paris, corn starch, etc., etc., have been mixed with various vehicles
and rubbed into the wood with but indifferent success. Most of
these compounds labor under the disadvantages of forming chemical compounds with the oil and consequently they shrink very
much on drying, so that though the surface may appear smooth
when they are first put on, waves and hollows make their appearance as they dry. These waves having round edges, are difficult
to fill, the second coat building up as much or more upon the
level spaces as in the hollows. It sometimes seems almost impossible with these fillers in the latter coats to make the hollows
hold any substance, the filler clinging chiefly to the surfaces.

I have thought it necessary to show how the ordinary or home-
made fillers act, and fail in order to show by contrast how much
easier it is to work efficiently with the mineral fillers. The mineral quartz; when mixed with oil, probably shrinks less in drying
than any other similar known mixture. If a surface of wood be
covered with this and then rubbed, the sharp and angular particles of the silica imbed themselves in the pores of the wood, closing them up, while the oil cements them fast. This is the foundation of Wheeler's wood filler, and which we recommend for
use by all wood finishers. When the pores have been filled
with the silica, and are cemented fast by the proper mixture of
gums and oils, the difficult part of the work is done.

After a good surface has been made upon the article it is ready
for the filler, which is to be selected according to the color desired. In putting the filler on it is thinned with turpentine until
about like flowing varnish, and is applied with a brush. Only so
much of the surface is covered as can be cleaned off before it
hardens. When it has set so that the gloss has left the surface, it
is at once rubbed off with " excelsior " or shavings, going across

the grain with the strokes.   If the filler dries too fast or too light
a little raw linseed oil may be used in it.

For a nicer job the filler is rubbed in with a rubber, made by
gluing a piece of sole or belt leather on the face of a block of
wood and trimming the edges flush with the block.   The rubbing
is done after the filler has set and before it is cleaned off.   If it
dries off too light, a little white japan may be added on nice
work.   The light-colored filler should be used on all work where
light and dark woods are used together.   The filling, it must be
understood, is done by the silica, which will often be found in
the shape of a sediment in the bottom of the mixture.   Eight
hours is generally considered a sufficient time for the filler to
dry.

When the work with the filler is done the surface of the wood
ought to be like so much ground glass.   Such portions of the
wood as show a solid grain need very little filler.   On Georgia
pine, after the filler is dry, a little rubbing in the direction of the
grain with very fine sand-paper is an advantage.   If the filler has
been properly used the desired results will be obtained with little
labor.

The wood is now in a condition to receive the final coat-
ings.   Whether the work is to be polished or "dead finished,"
do not employ shellac or "French polish."   If a "dead" surface is wanted, wax finish is easily put on, and as easily rubbed to
a good surface.   F. W. Devoe & Co. prepare a wax finish,
which is a convenient preparation of wax and gums, and can be
applied with a brush and then rubbed down with a woolen cloth,
tied up to make a hard rubber, until a fine lusterless surface is obtained.   With mahogany and similiar woods this greatly improves the color of the wood.   When this has dried, which will be
in the course of a few hours, the work is ready for use.   The wax
finish, like many of the furniture creams, has the advantage that it
can be put on in a few minutes at any time to brighten up work when
it has become dull.   A piece of work prepared in this way, after

four operations, will present as fine an appearance as the best cabinet work found in the furniture stores.

The materials which have been described, it will be noticed, are both manufactured articles. The prepared filler is indispensable ; the wax finish can be made by the mixing together, by the aid of heat, white wax and spirits of turpentine until they are of the consistency of thick paste. Another wax finish is made of beeswax, spirits of turpentine and linseed oil in equal parts The addition of two drams of Alkanet root to every twenty ounces of turpentine darkens and enriches the color. The root is to be put into a little bag and allowed to stand in the turpentine until it is sufficiently colored.

An altogether more durable surface can be made by a little change in the treatment. When the wood is filled instead of applying the wax, take some hard oil finish, a preparation manufactured by Messrs. Berry Bros., of Detroit, Mich., and put it on with a brush precisely like varnish. The coat should not be too heavy, especially on vertical surfaces, and the brush used ought to be a good one. This material gives a most brilliant polish. By rubbing it down with a woolen cloth and pumice stone powder it can also be made dull. Hard-oil finish does not spot with hot or cold water, is slightly elastic and is not injured by pretty severe soaking in water. It gets hard in twelve hours or less in warm weather and over night in winter time. It is one of the best surfaces which can be used, and has the advantage of working very well in the hands of one who is not an expert in the art of finishing wood or handling varnish. It will make a very fair surface applied direct to the unfilled wood, in which case it is a good substitute for shellac.

Wax finish has the advantage that scratches can be easily repaired without sending to the cabinet maker or the painter. Here a word of advice to the carpenter who does any work of this character may save him some trouble and make way for the further use of the same kind of finish. When the woodwork of a house is treated in this way, be sure and leave a little bottle of the wax polish with the housekeeper, with directions as to the method of using it. In sending out a "what-not," book-case, or any other article of similar kind, put up a little bottle of the polish and show the owner, or, preferably the lady of the house, how to repair any little scratch and make the work look "as good as new." The fresh appearance of the work will be a good advertisement, while it will prevent complaints and dissatisfaction that often follow the use of work which, when injured, cannot be restored.

It may be said that either of the methods of finishing involves a great deal of labor. This is true ; but the amount is not much greater than is needed for three coats of paint, and the cost of the paint would probably be more than the cost of the finish. The labor in one case can be of a cheap character, and in the other an experienced painter must be employed. The profit upon the "dead finish" can go into the pocket of the carpenter, while that of the painting must in any event be divided between the carpenter and painter, or belong to the latter altogether who is, after all the proper person to do the work.

I have now said about all that is necessary in the matter of "fillers" and "filling," but, as sometimes happens, the old system of "sizing," has to be resorted to for certain kinds of work, I give herewith a formula for its construction and use :

Size of different kinds is sometimes applied to the surface of wood to prevent absorption of the varnish. The kind of material used for the size is not important, the object being only to prevent absorption by a very thin coat of some substance not soluble in the varnish. For dark-colored wood, thin size, made by reducing ordinary glue with water, is generally used ; but for lighter-colored surfaces a white size is used, which is prepared by boiling white kid or other leather or parchment-cuttings, in water for a few hours, or until it forms a thin jelly like substance, which is reduced with water to a thin consistency, and used in a tepid state. Sometimes solutions of isinglass or tragacanth are employed in like manner. Unlike the best fillers, sizes of any kind do not improve the finish, and are sometimes a positive detriment to it. They are used solely as an economy to reduce the quantity of the varnish needed ; and their use is not recommended for the best work.

STAINING, FINISHING, VARNISHING AND POLISHING.

The following will apply to nearly all stained work with the exception that the coloring materials must be chosen to suit the results desired ; directions for mixing and preparing will be found under the head of woods.

Staining, or dyeing, though not very modern, has grown in popularity of late. This is due not so much to the natural imitation of valuable wood as to the beautiful colors in which it may be produced—for example, the deep red, generally represented as mahogany, which forms a handsome and lively contrast with nearly any color or style of finishing. In house interiors, however, it has not been so extensively used as it has on furniture, owing to the preference for the light wood for house finishing. But, despite its handsome color, at the present time it is obliged to yield to the more artistic and substantial old oak, which, it is generally anticipated, will continue in vogue a greater length of time than did the stained work. An objection to stained work is that after it has been in service a comparatively short time the finish and stain wear off from those portions most exposed to severe usage. The appearance is thereby destroyed, and it cannot be restored by refinishing. Another objection to stains is that they fade, a fault to which all these bright colors are subject.

Whether this style of work is *la mode* or not, it will always remain in greater or less demand. A few details of staining will, therefore, be due. Now, if the object of staining is to imitate natural wood, it would be found desirable to procure specimens of the woods to be imitated. Excellent and most convenient specimens can be obtained at any scroll-saw supply house at a trifling expense. Commence by oiling and varnishing the specimen to bring out the color, or apply a darkener if an antique

color is required. As a darkener for cherry, apply with a brush
aqua-ammonia diluted with water according to the depth of
color required. This is probably the best mixture for all red
woods, as it develops the colors to their utmost intensity. Lime·
water and lye (potash solution) are also frequently used, although
lye should be used cautiously; for if applied too strong, it
destroys the red color after developing it. Iron fillings or
shavings boiled in vinegar produce a darkener for oak, and are
frequently employed in producing the "darks" or shades in
sixteenth century finish.

After darkening with a water solution the specimens should not
be oiled, but after having thoroughly dried should receive a
coat of shellac, and, when dry, a coat of varnish. Having the
colors well brought out, they will be found of great utility in preparing a stain of accurate shade. Now, the secret in preparing a
good stain is that it should be perfectly transparent, which may
be produced in either oil or water colors. The latter, however,
with a few exceptions, will be found to give the best results, for
several reasons. In the first place, it penetrates deeper into the
wood, thus producing a more substantial finish. Next, the wood
employed is generally hard and fine, and by an application of
water stain the grain is raised, whereby the "lights" or veins
are more prominently brought out, imparting to the finish a more
vivid appearance, which cannot be so effectually produced in
oil colors. Still another advantage in water stain is the saving of
time in its application; for when properly prepared, it can be used
for dipping, which is the method practised in our cabinet shops
for staining much furniture. It can also be applied with
a brush, although good results by this method are accomplished
only when skill and practice are exercised. In applying it a four
or-five-inch flat bristle brush would be found the right size, ena-
bling the operator to cover over any one part or section before the
stain penetrates the wood. It will be found less difficult to apply
oil stain uniformly with a brush, and it is, therefore, generally employed in staining soft-wood and especially the different species

of pine, all of which absorb water stain in spots, giving it a daubed appearance.

The first thing to be considered is the receptacle or vessel in which the water or acid stains are to be prepared. This should be formed of a material which is unaffected by the corrosive action of acid. Porcelain-lined iron or glazed earthenware in the way of kettles or common stew crockery are commonly used. As the latter are often cracked by the heat required in boiling, it is safer and cheaper in the end to use porcelain-lined kettles.

I need not say that care and cleanliness are two very necessary qualities in the preparation and application of stains, for a good workman is always a careful and a clean workman.

In finishing "rubbing" may be considered one of the most essential qualities, since it gives to the varnish when laid upon the wood a degree of smoothness not otherwise attainable; for by the use of the brush alone minute furrows and ridges are left upon the plastic surface of the varnish, and although good varnish possesses in itself a high gloss, the gloss is not nearly so agreeable to the eye as the brilliant polish of which rubbing is the preliminary. The reduction of these ridges and furrows is accomplished by means of finely-powdered pumice-stone moistened with raw linseed oil, applied with a piece of haircloth or other coarse and fibrous material. For rubbing large flat surfaces the haircloth is sometimes folded over a block of convenient size, but this is not practicable for articles of small size or irregular shape. In rubbing, considerable force must be used, but the stroke must be steady, and as long as possible, and great care should be taken to rub the surface uniformly, as in case it is rubbed unevenly the varnish is liable to be worn away quite to the wood in some places, and the perfect smoothness that is the beauty of a good finish will thus be impossible. The edges especially are liable to be rubbed bare, and should be carefully treated. The crevices and hollows of carvings are rubbed by means of hard-pointed sticks of various convenient sizes. The rubbing should be continued until the entire surface appears perfectly smooth and free from marks of any kind. The surplus pumice-stone and oil should all be carefully removed from the surface by means of rags, and the work may then be cleaned up with a little sweet oil well rubbed in, and retouched with a cloth slightly dampened in alcohol, which serves to remove any remaining oil from the surface. If the article has veneered panels they are now ready for the final processes of "polishing," or "flowing," processes, whatever the kind of "finishing," the workman should make it a point where possible, to have a suitable temperature. No good finishing can be done under 60°, and it is hard to get the temperature too high for this work. The wood should be warm and perfectly dry, and visitors, flies, dirt, dust and dampness should rigorously be excluded from the room while the work is in progress.

The word "shellacking" has become of late very common with finishers and is often applied to first coating or "sizing," whether shellac be used or not. This, doubtless, arises from the fact of the general employment of shellac for first coating and up to the present time has proved the most suitable medium discovered for the purpose. I again quote from R. A. Bahre's papers on this subject.

Before proceeding with the application of shellac, it will be necessary to investigate the condition of the surface of the wood, taking care that no successive application is made before the preceding one is perfectly dry.

The dry condition of water-stained work may easily be determined by the uniformily dead appearance it presents, especially in the corners and angles. A surface treated with oil stain, when dry, will impart no color to the finger if brought in contact, and is effected in twelve or fifteen hours according to the amount of japan used.

The condition of a filled surface cannot be so readily observed, for in wiping off the filler from the surface, the moisture is likewise wiped off, and the surface is dry to the touch. But let us examine the pores, which have become small receptacles filled to the brim with a fatty substance. We find that the bulk of the substance in these pores does not dry so fast as were it spread out in a thin layer upon an extended surface. When regard is not paid to this condition and the surface is prematurely coated, it will be but a matter of a short time before the effects will become manifest by the cracking of the varnish, caused by the varnish becoming dry before the filler. We shall have something more to say on this subject later.

The safest way to ascertain whether a filler has become perfectly dry is to drop, while filling, a few drops upon a board and let them remain until they become hard enough to resist the pressure of the finger nail. The length of time required will depend upon the amount of oil contained in the filler.

Upon acquiring this degree of hardness the filler in the work may be considered dry, and ready to receive the first coating. This coating, which should be employed on all first-class work, is an alcoholic solution of gum shellac.

Among the advantages of this solution are, first, that it dries very rapidly, thus preventing it penetrating and sinking into the pores. Besides levelling the surface, it forms a close impenetrable body for receiving the varnish. By reason of this property it is also used for sealing up the pores of fine grained wood by applying two coats. On account of its best solvent (alcohol), it is indispensable for developing, certain stains, especially the aniline and other water stains which do not contain lye or glue. Alcohol does not affect the stains nor the glue ; for this reason an alkali stain should first receive a light coat of oil, while the glue stains require a strong glue size for their development.

The second advantage of shellac solution is its exceedingly hard drying qualities ; as it dries in five or six hours sufficiently hard to sandpaper, and in eight or ten hours becomes so hard that the finger nail can make no impression upon it, the surface is then ready for the second coat. In addition to this, its quality of hardness makes it indispensable for the first coating of all resinous woods, especially the pines, of which it not only seals up the pores but prevents the exudation of the resin while it sand-papers as fine as satin.

In preparing shellac for general use, dissolve in a gallon of alcohol (ethylic alcohol, spirits of wine) four pounds of the orange or five pounds of the white shellac, using the white upon light wood if a clean or clear job is required, and the orange if the color is immaterial or is required to be darkened, as the cost of the orange gum is about forty per. cent. less. The clearness of the orange gum depends much upon its freshness, and it is there-fore undesirable to prepare it until it is wanted for use, when the dissolving of the gum can be accelerated by warming and con-tinually agitating the mixture. Wood spirit (methylic alcohol) also dissolves this gum and is frequently substituted for pure alcohol, its cost being about one-third; but on account of dis-agreeable odor and deleterious effect it is rejected for first-class work.

The application of shellac is to an experienced finisher the most agreeable and least difficult part of finishing; but to a be-ginner it is often most aggravating and discouraging, it being very difficult to prevent lapping or doubling up. Especially is this the case when the lac is darker than the wood, as, for in-stance, in shellacking pine shutters with orange shellac, when the attempt of the beginner usually results in a total botch. An ex-perienced hand will produce a clear and even effect by proceed-ing in the following manner: Having in view the fact that the wood is very soft, he will dilute his lac somewhat with the spirits, to make it work free. Then, with a double-thick flat-chiselled bristle brush about two inches wide he will apply a very free coat to the closed slats, on the bar side, including the small ogee edge of the frame, taking care to daub none on the flat surface. Then, quickly turning to the other side and opening the slats, he will finish and lay off the sides, and, again closing the slats, proceed by coating them upon the plain (non-bar) sides, including the other edge of the frame. He will then return to the bar side, open, lay off and finish; then, running the brush up and down the bar, complete that portion of the work. It may be laid down as a rule that one section should be completed before another is started. When one portion is coated, proceed with the frame by coating the outside edges and then the centre rail, cutting the joints clean. Then begin at one end of the style and follow around until the starting-point is reached, being always careful to complete as you go on.

It is sometimes required to finish shutters in a hanging condition, but, on account of the speed required in applying the shellac, there is much danger of spattering the walls or windows. If, therefore, they are hung with loose joint butts, it will be found economical to remove them and finish them in a separate room.

We have thus far referred to the shellacking of pine shutters with orange shellac. If one has acquired proficiency in this point, all the remainder will come very easy to him, especially when using white shellac (transparent), which does not show the laps after varnishing. The whole secret of shellacking may be condensed in adherence to the following simple rules : First, to keep a wet edge to work to; second, always to work to a joint before stopping ; and third, never to repeat with the brush after becoming partly set, thereby causing it to "double up."

There are several substitutes for shellac, but the operator should remember they are only "substitutes," and cannot compare with the "real thing" and only the man who takes his work at starvation prices, will use the "subs," unless such be specified.

Oil shellac, which is used to a great extent, is generally supposed to be gum shellac dissolved in a volatile oil, and in quality virtually equal to alcohol shellac. This supposition is wrong however, for the gums employed are of an inferior sort, being chiefly taken from our pines and dissolved in turpentine or naphtha, and having a little linseed oil and chemical dryer thrown in. When dry it is very brittle, easily spoils and will not resist the action of water on the grain, and is utterly useless as a substantial finish. This so-called shellac, is applied in the same manner as varnish.

3

Glue size proves most effectual in holding out varnish, and while the work is new, it is not easily marred. In the course of two or three years, however, the glue decays, when the slightest bruise causes the varnish, size and all to give. For developing water-stains containing alkali it is quite effective.

"Hard oil finish" so-called, is simply an application of a quick-drying brittle varnish, that will polish with rubbing ; for inside work it contains very little "oil" while that prepared for outside purposes, contains more "oil," is more expensive, dries slower and is more durable.

It matters but little whether we employ shellac or a substitute, or even varnish for first coating. It should be allowed to dry and then receive a rubbing to take off all the grit or roughness which may have been caused by a little filler remaining on the surface or dust settled upon it before dry. Whatever it may be, it should be smoothed before applying a coat of varnish. For this purpose No. o sandpaper will be found the best adapted, but, as the ordinary sandpaper is very heavy, and therefore stiff, we are liable to cut through the edge in using it. Neither does it conform easily to mouldings and corners. It is therefore advisable to employ the thin paper especially prepared for the purpose ; but if it cannot be obtained, the heavy should be split—that is, by detaching one or two layers of the back paper. This can be accomplished in the following manner : Hold one corner of the sheet between the thumb and forefinger ; rub that corner briskly with a moistened finger of the other hand, and the layers will then become detached and can easily be separated by running the finger down the edge between the two layers. Then, holding the paper down upon a flat surface, the layers can be drawn asunder across the whole width of the sheet. By tearing the sheet once lengthwise and twice crosswise, we have pieces of a convenient size for use. As new paper scratches more or less, it will be advisable to rub the grit off upon another piece ; then by moistening the back we are able conveniently to get into the corners without scouring the edges through. Should the sandpaper still scratch (which it frequently does when inferior stock is used for coating), haircloth will do instead, using the hair side on the surface. This can be obtained at any furniture repair shop.

A very important part of hardwood finishing is the varnishing. Simple as it looks, it is extremely difficult to properly lay on a coat of varnish, and experienced varnishers will tell us that this is so. Scarcely two varnishers work alike, and it takes time and patient experience with any particular varnish to learn its peculiarities. We cannot teach how the varnishing should be done, but we can give a few general directions that may prove helpful. In the first place, do not be afraid of your varnish ; do not get excited if it threatens to give trouble. I have seen a carriage-painter tremble so when applying a strange varnish that he appeared as though in an ague-fit, and it is needless to say that it was a bad job. Apply the varnish quickly and freely, and do not work it much; the less varnish is worked after being applied, the higher will be the lustre. Remember this, for it is true and very important to know. Flow it on freely with a flat brush of suitable width, and use a badger or fitch hair brush ; a fine elastic or half-elastic chiselled bristle brush is very good. I mention the badger and the fitch more because they will outwear any bristle varnish brush and of course are cheaper.

A pound or any other bristle brush will answer for varnishing grained or painted work, on which the varnish is generally scrubbed, but in varnishing natural wood it should be laid on so as to level the surface, for which purpose fine-haired brushes are necessary.

Having the surface of the wood filled and shellacked, we have a ground-work suitable for any class of work from piano polish to cheap one-coat work. In selecting the varnish for the latter— which is generally left in the gloss—use a " finishing " varnish ; that is, a varnish retaining a bright gloss when dry. However, the varnishes with the brightest gloss are generally not very durable. When successive coats are to be applied either in oil—finishing—*i. e.*, oil rubbing—or polishing, a varnish is required that dries hard, but not brittle, the latter especially being characteristic of cheap gum varnish, such as colophony—common pitch or rosin—poor copal, etc. If the varnish contains much oil, it will render it elastic, making it difficult to rub; and therefore a good rubbing varnish should be made either of amber or of copal, the former being especially adapted to the manufacture of polishing varnish, as the gum is susceptible of a very fine polish. Varnishes to suit almost any purpose are generally obtainable at the dealers. We never can expect good results if we put a hard varnish over an elastic one or apply a coat before the previous one is dry. These are the main causes for varnishing cracking. The same trouble also arises when varnish is applied too heavily, so that the coat forms an enamel on the surface, remaining soft underneath, and then drying very slowly. While drying, the surface enamel contracts, consequently drawing the cracks open quite wide.

It is impossible to lay down rules which by simply being read would make a practical varnisher of a person, as varnishing requires much judgment and practice, but a few "tips" may not go amiss; at any rate, they assist in completing the subject.

We will now enter a room that has been sandpapered as described previously, having a temperature of about seventy degrees. We sprinkle with water, not flooding the floor, as a very damp atmosphere would prove injurious to the gloss of the varnish, then with a painter's duster carefully dust off all the work. This generally ends the preparation, but in order to remove all the dust it requires wiping off with a damp chamois skin; and when all is clean and dry, we are ready for the varnish. For a bucket or pot use one of the clean tin pails known as "two-quart-lunch pails." Then, to prevent the varnish from running down the outside by scraping the brush over the edge, a bar should be soldered across the pail about ½ inch from the top and a little on one side from the centre. Manufacturers claim that varnish should be used just as it is sold, and we find that nearly all good quality of varnishes work freely without diluting, but how to obtain good results with some of their cheap stuff without diluting remains a mystery to finishers. If, therefore, the varnish is of a poor, thick quality, add turpentine until it spreads freely with your " fitch brush," which, if the work is very complicated, should be two inches in width ; and if the work be plain, a three-inch could be used to advantage. Varnish should be applied freely—or, rather, flowed on, and not rubbed out, or " skinned " on, as finishers term it. In applying the varnish, first run freely over a panel, then run over it crosswise. If there are projections rising with an angle, or any grooves or depressions, as in mouldings, they will retain more varnish than the flat surface, and to prevent running down in them it requires drawing out. This is done by stabbing the brush into the angles and at the same time drawing it out toward the flat surface ; and when this is done, the whole length of the angle, we finish by laying off up and down. This should complete this portion of the work without being obliged to touch it again, and thus proceeding until a section of panels have been finished, when the frame should be gone over. In coating the panels the surface of the frame is very often daubed—in fact this is nearly inevitable—and to coat over this would form fat edges ; so we shall again make it fluid by mixing it with the fresh varnish, and this is done by " pounding " it up well—or, as a painter would call it, " stabbing " it—when it can be evenly laid off. The amount a surface will hold without running can be ascertained only by experience and judgment ; although much depends upon the way it is laid off, as a greater quantity can be applied if laid off up and down than horizontally, as the brushmarks give occasion for the varnish to " sag." But if such should take place after the varnish is partly set, it could be stopped by stabbing with the brush rubbed out dry, although this will leave the surface pitted, but, at any rate, much easier to rub out than a run. The brushes, when not in use, should be kept in varnish or washed out clean, which can be done by rubbing them out well with kerosene and then washing them with soap and water until perfectly clean.

Should it be desired after applying one coat of varnish, to proceed with the oil finish, that is "oil rubbing or polishing," we should first take into consideration the condition of our surface. Providing that one coat has filled the little depressions of the grain to a perfect level, we are prepared to proceed with the rubbing ; but this levelling is seldom effected with one coat, requiring, as a rule, at least two coats for fine wood and three or four coats for coarse-grained woods. The main object, however, is to form a coating sufficiently heavy to prevent rubbing it entirely off from the elevations in getting it down to that in the depressions.

As to the best method of rubbing and polishing as much or more diversity of opinion exists than in any other branch of the trade. This is probably due to the scheming and experimenting of the so-called "rushers," who get nervous at seeing a man take sufficient time to rub down a surface, and thus devise some new plan for hustling out the work, and generally, when the gloss is removed, the job is completed regardless of appearance. But nevertheless in all of these snide finishes there is generally a point or two of importance for us. We have for instance, a dead finish produced by adding wax to varnish. This is made by scraping the wax fine, putting it into a dish and covering it with a good turpentine japan placed over a fire to dissolve, but with a moderate heat. When dissolved, add twice its amount of varnish and apply with a fitch flowing brush. Although this does not produce a rubbed finish, it produces quite a clever imitation, and we can use it to advantage on the slats of shutters and on elaborately carved capitals, etc. It is not infrequently employed in floor finishing.

There is a method practised which removes the gloss from the varnish by rubbing with a mixture of oil and pumice-stone applied with a furniture scrub brush, or, for a large flat surface, a commercial stencil brush—No. 12 or 14 is frequently used—dipping the brush into the mixture and scrubbing it on to the surface; three or four scrubs are generally sufficient, depending particularly upon the cleaning off with wadding completely to remove the grass. Unless the varnish has been very cleanly applied and is perfectly level, it does not amount to much, for it does not smooth the surface.

Others, again, first sandpaper the surface with fine sandpaper, then rub it a trifle with oil and pumice, using a piece of burlap or old felt boot for a rubber. The only way yet discovered by which to level the surface is to rub it down with felt. For this operation we provide ourselves with a set of rubbers which may be made as follows: First take a piece of white Spanish felt one inch thick and about 3x5 in size; split it in two, and keep one half for the large plain surfaces. Then again split the other half, obtaining two thin pieces, reserving one for mouldings, etc., to which it will easily conform. We now want some tools to get into small corners so we whittle sticks about six or eight inches long and in shape of a triangle, half round and oblong; then, cutting the ends square, glue a piece of thin felt upon it, allowing the glue to dry thoroughly before putting in oil. For getting around in the bottom of carvings, we whittle a stick of basswood bark, and, moistening it, stub the end to a pulp. A scrub brush will also be necessary to remove the gloss from the beads and around the edges of the panels, etc. The oil generally used for rubbing is golden oil, known as machine oil, although crude petroleum, raw linseed and cotton seed oils are often used, but none of the latter cut so rapidly or clean off so well as the golden.

Pumice-stone No. o is generally used, although some prefer No. oo or ooo, but these are quite fine, and therefore do not cut very fast. In applying the oil and pumice, some prefer dipping the rubber first into the oil, then into the powder, and thus convey it to the surface, while others apply the oil with a piece of wadding, then sprinkle on the powder.

To excel in rubbing, like all other branches of the trade, requires practice, always remembering that if the rubber is allowed to lag over the edge while drawing back and forward it will rub the edge through. And, furthermore, the work should always be rubbed lengthwise the grain, so if it be necessary at the ends of panels next to the rails, where it is generally inclined to be rough, to rub crosswise, it should be rubbed down crosswise, but finished lengthwise, to take away the scratchy appearance. Before attempting to rub, the varnish should resist the impression of the finger-nail, or when rubbed before dry it will again flow, causing bright spots to reappear, generally known as "sweating," and would require re-rubbing after becoming dry. An experienced hand could easily tell when his surface was sufficiently rubbed by raising the felt or edge and drawing a clean streak the length of the work, and if the surface has lost its pitted appearance the rubbing is complete and ready to be cleaned off. This is accomplished easier if done directly, not allowing the oil to soak and soften the varnish, which causes the surface to appear mottled and smeary.

In cleaning use fine softwood sawdust, moistened a trifle to prevent scratching; and when the bulk of the oil is removed, the corners picked out and the work dusted it is again wiped off with wadding or waste, splitting the sheets of wadding to get the soft inside, then with the point of a pick and the wadding the beads and corners are carefully freed from all particles of oil and pumice. Should there be sags and runs or wrinkles which the ordinary rubbing did not remove, they should be rubbed out with pumice and strong soapsuds, then rubbed over a little with the oil again.

It is often required, in finishing a job, to form a contrast by polishing the raise of the panels, thus producing a rich and elegant finish.

In polishing as well as rubbing the hustlers have their schemes. One scheme commonly practised is, after the ordinary oil rubbing, to rub the surface to be polished with a bunch of raw cotton moistened with about equal parts of sweet oil and alcohol, the oil and spirits being put into a bottle and well shaken before moistening the cotton. Although this may be a hustler's scheme, an experienced hand with it can produce elegant results. In hand polishing proceed somewhat differently. First complete the oil rubbing, omitting the parts to be polished, then proceed by rubbing those parts with pumice and water, using pumice for that purpose, levelling the surface as much as the coating will permit, then cleaning off with damp chamois frequently rinsed in clean water. We then apply a coat of polishing varnish, which, when dry, is again rubbed down with pumice flour and water, using a fine but soft piece of felt ; and when perfectly smooth, it is carefully cleaned off, so that none of the pumice remains upon the surface, as this will scratch and destroy the polish. It is then rubbed again with rotten stone and a piece of chamois leather, using the lump of rotten stone and changing the rubber by rubbing it over the lump three or four times, then rubbing the surface quite briskly, for in this rubbing is where the polishing really is done. This powder then is allowed to dry upon the surface, and then with a short circular motion with the ball of the hand we proceed to rub off the powder, frequently wiping the hand upon a rag free from all other dust or pumice-stone. Then, if the varnish was of a superior quality, the polish is complete; but should the varnish contain cheap gum or a too great amount of oil, it is nearly impossible to produce a bright polish, although in this case the method first mentioned would prove quite effective—viz., that of using an old silk handkerchief to rub with in place of the cotton.

In the finest sort of general work, get a good quality of carriage varnish, and be sure and, do not *mix* either *oil or turpentine* with it, as it is prepared and put up for immediate use and specially prepared to meet special needs. Two coats of varnish are usually sufficient when the filling has been complete. When the first coat is dry, rub it down with pulverized pumice-stone and water—in some cases simply with curled hair, which removes the gloss and makes a good finishing-coat possible. The rubbing accomplished, wash and dust off well; then apply the finishing-coat of varnish. If a "polished" surface be required, the last coat must be rubbed down as before with pumice-stone and brought to a mirror-like surface with rotten-stone and water. Clear up with a little sweet oil, and afterward with a cloth dampened with alcohol. A "dead finish" is produced by rubbing the varnished surface with powdered pumice-stone and raw linseed oil, which gives a semi-lustrous finish of great beauty and durability. Another method of polishing hardwood is described as follows: Take a long piece of list or coarse flannel and roll it up in a wad like a roll of rope, and over this wrap a soft piece of linen several times doubled up; sew it on tightly and form a sort of handle by tying up a round wad. Then put into a saucer some shellac varnish, into which dip the flat side of the wad until it becomes saturated. Pouring a few drops of boiled linseed oil on the face of the wad, rub the work briskly and lightly in a circular direction, doing a small space at a time until the whole surface is gone over. Repeat the operation, allowing each successive application to dry well, or rubbing dry and not putting on too much polishing-liquid at a time.

Observe cleanliness and care during these operations. Such parts as cannot well be reached with the wad polish with a bit of flannel. This will give a very durable polish, and the parts are readily brightened up at any time by means of flannel moistened with oil. Remember that in all these operations the utmost care and patience must be exercised if one would have a perfect job. Do not slight the work in the minutest particular. Take your time and do everything as it should be done, filling in well, rubbing down smoothly and dusting off carefully.

A term sometimes used by American workmen is somewhat misleading; I refer to the word "flowing," as applied to varnishing. The term is given to the process of giving the work, after it has been properly prepared, a coat of varnish made expressly for that purpose, called "flowing varnish." The process as so named, as given herewith is quoted from an English authority:

Veneered panels are usually finished that way. Some finishers, when the body-work is to be dead-finish with flowed panels, coat the panels with the same varnish—shellac or other—used for the body, and rub them with pumice-stone and oil; in fact, up to the point of flowing make no difference whatever in the treatment of the body-work and the panels. Such treatment is not recommended; whatever varnish is used for the body-work, the panels should be coated with two or three coats of the best rubbing varnish; oil should not be used for rubbing, as, if the surface is at all greasy, the subsequent coat of flowing varnish cannot be evenly laid, therefore water should be used with the pumice-stone for rubbing, in place of oil. After the rubbing is completed, wash off with a sponge, and dry with a chamois skin. Let it stand for a day, and after freeing the work from all pumice-stone and dust, taking it to the flowing-room, which should be clean, dry, and free from all draughts of air, apply the varnish with a flat brush of suitable width, made of badger or fitch hair; lay the varnish on smoothly and evenly, leaving no marks of the brush. The quicker the varnish is put on, and the less it is worked, the better it will look. Let it stand in the room until it is hard enough to handle. Upholstered work should not be flowed until it comes from the hands of the upholsterer and is ready for the ware-rooms.

Varnish polishing is used when it is desired to give to the work a bright lustre, differing from the natural gloss, and resulting from a perfectly smooth surface produced by rubbing. The previously applied coats of rubbing varnish having been rubbed down with pumice-stone and water, one or more coats of polishing varnish are applied, rubbed down as before, and brought to a bright mirror-like surface with rotten-stone and water. Clean up with a little sweet oil, and afterward with a cloth damped in alcohol.

There are many makes of varnish in the market at the present writing, that are especially adapted for natural wood finish and which may be obtained from any respectable dealer. The most reliable manufacturers of varnish in the United States, whose preparations may be depended on to a dead certainty, do not number more than a half a dozen firms among which may be named Devoe & Co., of New York City, Murphy & Co., of New York, and Berry Bros., of Detroit, Mich. The Murphy Company make a transparent varnish that is extensively used in the trade. It is used for either a high polish or dead surface. It is recommended especially for developing the grain of natural wood ; for durability in all temperatures, freedom from discoloration from soap, water or acids, a perfect adherence to the surfaces, preventing cracking, flaking or blistering, while acting as a good preservative of the wood or metal, preventing either decay or rust.

It is made in different qualities, adapted to interior finishing on walls, floors or ceilings in halls, bath-rooms or kitchens for dwellings, asylums and hospitals, and also for exterior work, such as front doors, vestibules, window castings, and protecting the wood from weather exposure.

The Berry Bros. of Detroit, also make a white varnish that possesses all the requisites of a first-class finishing material. The preparations of Devoe & Co. are so well known and so universally used, that only a bare reference to them is necessary. Doubtless there are other makes of varnish that answer equally well with those named.

I think I have now placed before the reader pretty nearly all that is worth saying on the subject of hardwood and natural wood finish, and have drawn largely from the best authorities extant ; but it would not be wise to close this section, without giving as briefly as possible, a few rules on the now almost obsolete process of French polishing, as occasionally this method of finishing is employed for certain purposes :

French polishing is a method of varnishing by rubbing the varnish upon the surface of the wood instead of applying it with brushes. When varnish is applied simply with a brush, a comparatively uneven surface results, rendering necessary the subsequent process of rubbing and polishing, but by the method of

French polishing, a smooth and continuous, surface hard and not easily scratched, is secured.

All the polishes are applied very much in the same way, and a general description will therefore be sufficient. To obtain a good polish with lac varnish on wood, the quantity applied must be very small, and must be rubbed continuously until dry. If the work be porous or cross grained, it will be necessary to give it a coat of thin clear size previous to commencing with the polish ; when dry, the surface must be smoothed with fine glass or sand-paper. The size fills up the pores and saves the polish, and also saves considerable time in the operation.

Make a wad of cotton-batting, covered with several folds of very new fine soft linen cloth ; put the wad or cushion to the mouth of the bottle containing the preparation (or polish) and shake it sufficiently to damp the cloth ; then proceed to lightly rub the work with circular motion ; as the rubber becomes drier, the pressure may be increased, but care should be taken not to press too heavily when the rubber contains much polish, as a streakiness will result. The circular motion should be continued until the rubber becomes quite dry, when more polish may be taken upon it and the rubbing renewed. It should be borne in mind that the rubber should never be raised directly from the work, but should be raised with a sweeping motion ; also that it should never for a moment remain quiet upon the surface ; and that its motion should be as even as possible ; neglect of these precautions will produce a rough surface wherever the rubber remains quiet or is improperly removed. The circular rubbing must be continued until the surface appears perfectly smooth and the pores are no longer visible. Be very particular to keep the cloth covering of of the wad clean and soft ; it is desirable to use a clean portion each time it is dipped in the polish. It is quite likely that in about twelve hours after the above operation the surface of the work will be lustreless, and the grain plainly visible, in that case proceed over the work again until the grain is thoroughly filled. French polishing is a process requiring particular care and skill, and considerable experience is necessary to produce good results.

Beginners will find that they will be more successful with a flannel rubber, made in the shape of a ball. Most polishers use wadding, which is more pliable and better to get in the internal angles or small mouldings A bottle with a slit cork is the best to apply the polish to the rubber. In commencing, the rubber should not be rubbed quite dry, as you will never get any body on the work by so doing; but, as the shiny appearance advances, you must rub each rubber dry. Every time the rubber is wetted with polish it should be pressed in the palm of the left hand, which will equalize the polish. After the cover is put over, which should be some clean old cotton or print rags, the top of the finger should be dipped in linseed oil and applied to rubber-cover—just enough to keep it from sticking. As soon as the cover has a shiny appearance, it should be removed to a fresh place. As soon as the work has got a good body of polish on, it should be set away for at least ten hours, to allow for the polish to sink, which always takes place.

Before commencing to polish again, the work should be very carefully rubbed over with the finest glass-paper obtainable, taking care not to cut through the skin; then proceed as before. Be sure never to let the rubber stop in one place for an instant, as it will surely take off the polish to the bare wood and spoil the job. After the work has sufficient polish on, it should be allowed to stand three or four hours before spiriting off.

The same rubber will do; only use spirits. Just damp the rubber, and cover three or four times double with cover, and rub very lightly over the work; but care must be taken not to make the rubber too wet, or the work will be spoilt. The same process will answer for pine or deal, only no filling is required, but a coat of clean patent size, before applying the polish.

The ingredients for the above kind of work are quite numerous, but shellac, dissolved in alcohol, is the basis of all French polishes, and some finishers use thin shellac varnish without other admixture, slightly moistening the rubber with linseed oil to prevent stickiness and make it work smoothly. There is a great variety of admixtures and diversity in the proportion of ingredients, but the differences are not material. I subjoin a number of receipts.

First and Best.—To one pint of spirits of wine add a quarter of an ounce of gum-copal, a quarter of an ounce of gum-Arabic, and one ounce of shellac.

Let the gums be well bruised, and sifted through a piece of muslin. Put the spirits and the gums together in a vessel that can be closely corked; place them near a warm stove, and frequently shake them. In two or three days they will be dissolved. Strain the mixture through a piece of muslin, and keep it tight corked for use.

Next.—Take one ounce each of mastic, sandarac, seed lac, shellac, gumlac, and gum-Arabic; reduce them to powder; and add a quarter of an ounce of virgin wax; put the whole into a bottle, with one quart of rectified spirits of wine; let it stand twelve hours, and it will be fit for use.

Another.—Put into a glass bottle one ounce of gumlac, two drachms of mastic in drops, four drachms of sandarac, three ounces of shellac, and half an ounce of gum dragon; reduce the whole to powder; add to it a piece of camphor the size of a nut, and pour on it eight ounces of rectified spirits of wine. Stop the bottle close, but take care, when the gums are dissolving, that it is not more than half full. Place near a warm stove until dissolved.

Other French-Polish Receipts.—1 pint naphtha, 3½ ounces orange shellac, ½ ounce elima. Darken with red saunders wood.

To one pint of spirits of wine, add half an ounce of gum shellac, half an ounce of seed lac, and a quarter of an ounce of gum sandarac; submit the whole to a gentle heat, frequently shaking it, till the various gums are dissolved, when it is fit for use.

Shellac, 6 ounces; naptha, 1 quart; sandarac, 1 ounce; benzoin, ¾ ounce.

Three ounces shellac, ½ ounce of gum mastic pulverized, and one pint of methylated spirits of wine added. Let it stand till dissolved.

Twelve ounces shellac, 2 ounces gum elima, 3 ounces gum copal, 1 gallon of spirits of wine; dissolve.

The following must be well mixed and dissolved:—Pale shellac, 2¼ pounds; 3 ounces mastic, 3 ounces sandarac, 1 gallon spirits of wine. After the above is dissolved, add 1 pint copal varnish, 1¼ ounces shellac, ½ ounce gum juniper, ½ ounce benzoin, ½ pint of methylated alcohol.

A Good Polish.—To a pint of spirits of wine add, in fine powder, one ounce seed lac, two drachms of gum guaiacum, two drachms of dragon's-blood, and two drachms of gum mastic; expose them, in a vessel stopped close, to a moderate heat for three hours, until you find the gums dissolved; strain the whole into a bottle for use, with a quarter of a gill of the best linseed oil, to be shaken up well with it.

This polish is more particularly intended for dark-colored woods—for it is apt to give a tinge to light ones, as satin-wood or air-wood, etc.—owing to the admixture of the dragon's-blood, which gives it a red appearance.

A Polish that Will Stand Water.—Take a pint of spirits of wine, two ounces of gum benzoin, a quarter of an ounce of gum sandarac, and a quarter of an ounce of gum anime; these must be put into a stopped bottle, and placed either in a sand-bath or in hot water till dissolved; then strain the mixture, and, after adding about a quarter of a gill of the best clear poppy oil, shake it well up, and put it by for use.

Prepared Spirits.—This preparation is useful for finishing after any of the foregoing receipts, as it adds to the lustre and durability, as well as removes every defect, of the other polishes; and it gives the surface a most brilliant appearance.

Half a pint of the very best rectified spirits of wine, two drachms of shellac, and two drachms of gum benzoin. Put these ingredients into a bottle, and keep it in a warm place till the gum is all dissolved, shaking it frequently; when cold, add two teaspoonfuls of the best clear white poppy oil; shake them well together, and it is fit for use.

This preparation is used in the same manner as the foregoing polishes; but, in order to remove all dull places, you may increase the pressure in rubbing.

Polish for Turner's Work.—Dissolve 1 ounce of sandarac in ½ pint of spirits of wine; shave 1 ounce of beeswax, and dissolve it in a sufficient quantity of spirits of turpentine to make it into a paste, add the former mixture to it by degrees; then, with a woollen cloth, apply it to the work while it is in motion in the lathe, and polish it with a soft linen rag; it will appear as if highly varnished.

A French Polish Reviver.—Beat gum acacia and white of two eggs in a mortar until they amalgamate; then add half a pint of raw linseed oil and best vinegar, eight ounces methylated spirits of wine, one ounce hydrochloric acid and two ounces muriate of antimony. They are to be rubbed on the surface of the furniture until dry, and will give a brilliant and lasting polish.

It now remains to explain the several varieties of finishing in use; these are largely derived from the peculiar qualities of the different varnishes used. Polishing varnishes, which are very hard and durable, are so called because their surface can be brought to a high lustre by rubbing with the proper materials. Flowing or finishing-varnishes contain more oil than polishing-varnishes, dry more slowly, and are softer, but their peculiar qualities are brilliancy and durability, fitting them for work requiring a brilliant gloss, such as veneered panels. Rubbing-varnishes are those that dry sufficiently hard to admit of being rubbed to a smooth surface. Turpentine varnishes, being the cheapest variety, are employed for cheap work, such as common chairs, bedsteads, &c.

Dead Finish is a term applied to the finish produced by the reduction of any of the rubbing varnishes with powdered pumicestone, and raw linseed oil, the surface thus produced being left in

4

the semi-lustrous state by omitting the polishing process. It is now more used than any other for body work, shellac varnish being generally employed because of its adaptation to the requirements of fine cabinet-work, and its properties of quick and hard drying. Copal, anime, and amber varnishes are also used, but are slower drying. The number of coats required depends somewhat upon the quality of the filler, but usually three coats, and sometimes less, are amply sufficient.

Varnish Finish.—For Cheap Work.—One coat of filler or stain followed by one coat of cheap turpentine varnish without rubbing. In this class of work the brilliancy of the gloss and covering qualities of the varnish are principally considered. The cheaper turpentine varnishes have a brilliant gloss, and dry very hard, but the gloss is not permanent, and after drying the gum is very brittle and easily cracked and broken. The gum is principally common resin.

Wax Finish.—Mix together, with heat, white wax, and spirits of turpentine to the consistency of thick paste ; when cold, apply it to the work with a rag ; rub on heavily so as to fill the pores of the wood ; remove all wax from the surface with a wooden scraper made in the shape of a carpenter's chisel ; smooth off with a bunch of soft rags by rubbing hard and quick for a few minutes ; finish with a little French polish applied with a cotton pad. For table tops and all large flat surfaces, allow the wax to remain on, and finish with a warm iron by passing it lightly and quickly over the work until the wax is made smooth and the surface is sufficiently polished. This is not considered a desirable finish, as it is not durable, and water spots it very easily.

The brushes required for varnishing are of many kinds and sizes and a description of even a portion of them, is out of the question in a small work of this kind ; however a few remarks concerning them may not be out of place. For spirit varnishes, camel's-hair pencils and brushes are used, the sizes of which vary from one-quarter to three-quarters of an inch diameter, according to the size of the work. When the surfaces are very large, flat camel-hair brushes are used ; but from their comparative thinness they scarcely contain a sufficient quantity of varnish to preserve the brush uniformly. charged in passing over a large sur-face. Turpentine and oil varnishes require less delicacy ; and flat brushes, made of fine soft bristles, are generally used, or sometimes ordinary painting brushes are employed, but they are rather harsh, and, owing to the adhesion of the varnish, the hairs are apt to be loosened, and come out. Brushes should al-ways be kept perfectly soft and clean, and therefore should never be laid aside when through work, without cleaning. For this purpose turpentine is best ; the brushes can either be washed out quite clean in it, dried on a cloth, and laid aside, or the bristles can be partially immersed in turpentine and allowed to remain in it until wanted for use. Warm water and soap will also serve to clean the brushes. If, however, the brushes are laid aside with-out being thoroughly cleaned, they will certainly be ruined by the hardening of the varnish.

Varnish pans can be procured at any varnish shop. They are constructed of tin, with a false bottom ; the interval between the two bottoms is filled with sand, which being heated over the fire keeps the varnish fluid, and it flows more readily from the brush. There is a tin handle to them, and the false bottom slopes from one end to the other, which gives sufficient depth when the varnish is low. They should also have a wire fixed across the top to wipe the brush against. An ordinary preserve jar is frequently used for containing the varnish, and is sufficiently suitable ; but it also should have a wire or string stretched across the top, for reducing the quantity of varnish taken up by the brush. The quantity of varnish poured into the jar should be sufficient to nearly cover the hairs of the brush in order to keep it soft. Too small a quantity of varnish is liable to thicken rapidly by evapo-ration, which should at all times be prevented as far as possible, by keeping the vessel closely covered when not in actual use.

The Various Woods, their Stains and Finish.—The foregoing rules and instructions apply, in a great measure to all woods that are to be finished in natural colors or stained, but under this head it is intended to take each wood separately, with regard to coloring, and other matters not before mentioned, that may be considered necessary to insure good work.

It should not be forgotten, when speaking of hard-wood finishing, that some of the prettiest woods used, are not " Hard " but soft woods among which may be mentioned pine of various kinds, poplar, cedar, red-wood, hemlock and basswood. When some of these are finished in their natural state or stained to imitate harder woods their beauty is much enhanced and they become deserving of more than a passing notice. Pine when properly prepared, is in my opinion one of the most useful as well as one of the prettiest woods that Nature has given to this continent, and hemlock which is a much despised wood, when properly prepared and finished in the natural state, or slightly " Mahoganized," makes the richest of panels for doors, wainscot or other house finish. As oak and mahogany are rivals as to which is the better and handsomer woods for finish, I will commence this section with those woods, giving oak the preference.

Oak.—We have in this country over forty kinds of oak nearly every one of which may be used for some special purpose, those most used for building finish and for furniture however are only few, among which are the white oak, (*Querus rulia*), rock oak (*Querus primas murticola*) and black oak (*Querus tindoris*). All of the above named oaks are capable of being handsomely finished, the white and black oaks being the best and the red being next.

What is known as quarter-oak is made by first sawing the log from end to end through the middle. Then each half is sawed from end to end through the middle, thus leaving four quarters. Each quarter has only three sides, one side the bulge part of the log, and the other two sides flat and coming to an edge. The boards are sawed off the sharp edge, and each sawing, therefore, throws off a board wider than one before it. Sawing the quarters of the log in this manner, lumber possesses that beatiful cross-

grained figure so much in fashion now that it has become somewhat of a craze. This cross-grained material finds favor in the
finest furniture and interior work. The wood is susceptible of the
very finest polish, and the cross-grain produces an effect made by
both nature and the saw, that is quite superior to the art of the
most skillful grainer. To effect a good imitation of antique oak
lamp black or Vandyke brown in oil is applied to the surface of
the wood, darkening its natural hue, but this is not by any means
best or the only way, but answers very well where other processes or methods are not available. With regard to giving oak an
antique appearance, many opinions exist. Formerly—and probably the first—imitations of antique oak were produced by ex-
posing the bare dressed surface to the steam of boiling ammonia.
This process, however, it was impossible to apply to casings of house
interiors, thus leading to the application of the aqua ammonia
with a brush, but, it is by repeated application that the desired results are produced. It stains the wood gray. There are
finishers who claim this to be the only process by which
to imitate Nature, but another much faster, and one which
gives the same results, is to use strong vinegar with iron
filings or shavings added ; by a little experimenting, this
can be made to suffice with one coat, depending upon the
amount of iron added.

A very clever imitation of the general antique can be obtained
by staining the filler with Vandyke brown and charcoal, equal
parts, using about one part of the colored to four parts of the
light. Then there is another antique which imitates certain oak
from the sixteenth century ; the peculiarity of it consists in dark
cloud streaks permeating the wood in every direction some of
them crossing the panels in a V-shape, others straight near top
and bottom. To give them an odd appearance, a pair of panels
can be clouded by streaking one three or four times and the other
once or twice. These stripes vary in width from three to five
inches. The wider streaks look well across the top of a table three
or four times, or even partly across, while the narrow ones would

do well around the legs and across the styles and rails of panelled work. In putting these on, they should be dark in the centre and blend out at the edges. This is done with an automatic paint burner, allowing the flames to scorch the wood nearly black ; but care must be taken not to char it. After the work is all streaked the wood is filled with filler stained with burnt umber mixed as for black walnut.

Care must be taken to have the filler stained to the proper tint, and in applying correctly. By following the rules given under the head "Filling" the operator should have no trouble in making good work, and we here repeat the instruction.

"After enough surface has been covered with the filler, so that what has been first applied begins to flatten, the process of wiping should immediately begin, using for that purpose either a rag or a handful of waste or excelsior. If the oak is very open-grained, waste is preferable. With a piece of this that has previously been used and is pretty well supplied with filler, rub crosswise of the grain, rather rubbing it into the grain than wiping it off. After the whole surface has been gone over in this way, take a clean piece of waste or rag (never use excelsior for wiping clean) and wipe the surface perfectly clean and free from filler, using a wooden pick, the point of which has been covered with a rag or waste to clean out the corners, beads, etc. It is well to give these picks some attention, as a person once accustomed to certain tools can accomplish more and better work than with tools that feel strange in his hands; therefore, each finisher should furnish his own pick. As to their construction, these are best made from second-growth hickory, which can be procured from any carriage repair shop, such as old spokes, broken felloes, etc. They are made eight inches in length, half inch oval at one end and tapering down to the point at the other. Sharpen the oval end like a coal chisel, then smooth with sandpaper, which should also be used to sharpen the tool when the same becomes worn dull.

This picking out of the filler from beads, etc., can be accelerated by the use of a picking brush manufactured especially for that purpose, but it is not advisable to use this on very coarse-grained oak, as it scrubs the filler out of the pores.

There are several fillers used which do not require this picking and scrubbing. One is a liquid filler used chiefly for carriage finishing; but it can be used successfully on butternut, bird's-eye maple, curly maple, satinwood, hickory, etc. It is made from gum and oil. Another is a filler made from finely-ground pumice stone, mixed as other fillers. It is applied with a brush, and must be left to dry at least twenty-four hours; it is then sand-papered smooth, when an oil varnish is applied, rendering it completely transparent. This last can be used only upon light wood.

It is a well-established fact that nearly all the oaks grow dark with age; many of them assume an entirely different shade from that which they have when new and first cut. For instance, light oak, when new, is of a sort of cream color; when aged in a dry atmosphere, it will assume a reddish brown, and in a damp atmosphere it will turn a gray with a blue tinge and eventually become brown. Cherry will turn from a light salmon to a maroon, and the same with mahogany. It has not been so long since mahogany and cherry were antiquated by being colored dark with stains or other coloring material, while, at the same time, oak was finished light. At present this manner of finishing is entirely reversed. Cherry, mahogany and all dark woods are finished as light as possible, while oak and ash, especially black ash, are finished antique.

Another method of rendering new oak wainscoting and other oak work dark, and give it an antique appearance is given.

A correspondent in the *English Mechanic* gives the following process of treatment, which he considers the best, after trying the various other processes used by builders and cabinet-makers to darken woods: " Oak is fumigated by liquid ammonia, strength 880°, which may be bought at any wholesale chemist's at 5s. a gallon. The wood should be placed in a *dark* and *air-tight* room (in a big packing case, if you like!), and half a pint or so of ammonia poured into a soup plate, and placed upon the *ground* in the center of the compartment. This done, shut the entrance, and secure any cracks, if any, by pasted slips of paper. Remember that the ammonia does not touch the oak, but the gas that comes from it acts in a wondrous manner upon the tannic acid in that wood, and browns it so deeply that a shaving or two may actually be taken off without removing the color. The depth of shade will entirely depend upon the quantity of ammonia used and the time the wood is exposed. Try an odd bit first experimentally, and then use your own judgment."

Short pieces of stuff may be so treated by using an air-tight box. The box ready, a flat dish or plate of strong ammonia should be placed in the bottom, so that the fumes will *rise* and surround the object. All that is now necessary is to place the article in the box, nailing up as close as possible and await results. Ten hours exposure using strong ammonia, should give a good color; if not dark enough let it remain longer, bearing in mind, however, that the wood will present no noticeable change until oiled or brought in contact with a wet substance such as shellac. It is well, therefore, to note the progress by touching the wood with the wet finger when it will show at once the stage it has reached.

There could be no better method devised to stain oak than this when practicable, and in adopting it we simply anticipate nature which in time through the action of the ammonia of the atmosphere would present the same result. Mahogany may also be treated similarly with success.

Here is another method of making antique oak, and I might add, that white, and black ash, and chestnut, similarly treated, will give a fair imitation of antique oak: The job should be made of hard wood, with as full an open grain as possible to secure a fine effect. Sandpaper this and clean off. Then prepare a priming made of 1 part japan, 1 part raw linseed oil and 1 part rubbing varnish. Drop into ½ gallon of the liquid 1 pound of commercial corn starch, such as is used for culinary purposes. Next take some good, dry, burnt Turkish umber, and add about ¼ pound of this to the starch. Apply to the job a good flowing coat of this priming. Let stand until it is set and has soaked well into the grain, and then take a broad putty knife and stick it into the grain, working the knife crosswise of the grain. Again let stand a little while, and then wipe with rags; especially clean out all the corners, and get the job into as good condition as possible as regards having the grain well filled.

Upon the completion of the operation above described it will be found that the open grain has absorbed the starch and umber, and that these portions now show the dark shade suggestive of age, while all the rest of the surface is also slightly darkened.

When again perfectly dry, give one coat of rubbing varnish, prepared by adding to it ½ pound of starch to each gallon of varnish. This coat should be flowed on freely as a medium coat of rubbing varnish, but be careful not to have runs of sags. This ought to completely fill the wood, after which proceed to varnish, rub and finish the job in the usual manner. To produce a natural oak finish, follow precisely the same course as above described, with the single exception of omitting the umber. This will leave the wood in its natural color.

Some of the most attractive work in this line, however, is effected by simply spreading on the surface of the material a concentrated solution of permanganate of potash, this being allowed to act until the desired shade is obtained. Five minutes suffice ordinarily to give a good color, a few trials indicating the proper proportions. The substance named is decomposed by the vegetable fibre with the precipitation of brown peroxide of manganese, which the influence of the potash, at the same time set free fixes in a durable manner on the fibres. When the action is terminated, the wood is carefully washed with water, dried, then oiled and polished in the usual manner. The effect produced by this process in several woods is really remarkable. On the cherry especially it develops a beautiful red color which well

resists the action of air and light, and on the other woods it has a
very pleasing and natural effect.

Along with the foregoing may be added the following stains for
oak : add to a quart of water 2 ounces each of potash and pearl-
ash. This is a very good stain, but it should be used carefully
as it blisters the hands and softens brushes. The stain may be
made lighter by adding more water.

Other Oak Stains.—To darken the color of oak any of the
following may be used :

Liquid ammonia laid on evenly with a rag or brush will
deepen the color immediately, and it will not fade, this being an
artificial production of result produced naturally by age.

Bichromate of potash, dissolved in cold water, and applied
with a brush, will produce a similar result.

A decoction of green walnut-shell will bring new oak to any
shade or nearly black.

Another.—To two quarts of boiled oil ; half a pound of ground
umber, mixed in oil by colorman ; one pint of liquid driers, stirred in ; one pint of turpentine ; mix. After cleaning and planing
your boards, lay this on with the grain of the wood. If required
lighter add naphtha till the required shade is attained ; it darkens
with age. Give it twelve hours to dry ; then varnish with wood
varnish, or use only beeswax and turpentine. The result is good
in time, but slower than varnish.

Mahogany.—(*Svietened.*)—The tree has a darkish-brown bark
and a reddish-brown, coarsely fibred, streaky, hard wood. The
tree grows to the height of 35 metres, and is pretty strong. The
chief varieties are the common mahogany, with a very hard, very
durable wood, which is never attacked by worms, and is excellent for ship-building ; but its capability for taking a fine polish
is its chief recommendation. *Mahagoni Haiti, Mahagoni Jam-
aika, Mahagoni Havanna* are the other chief kinds.

Thirty-five years ago mahogany was commercially designated as
"St. Domingo," from the island of St. Domingo, and "Baywood," or "Bay Mahogany," from the vicinity of the Bay of

Honduras, in Central America. The Central American wood was condemned as being too soft, of light weight, straight-grained and characterless. In recent years it has ceased coming to this market, but one cargo having arrived at the port of New York (the largest mahogany market in the world) in six years. St. Domingo mahogany likewise exists only in name, the original growth having long since been utilized ; only the small and stunted second growth being received here now. The individual logs of great size and best quality are so seldom found as to come within the category of " rare specimens. "

The Central American wood having been debarred by reason of softness, and the St. Domingo being virtually extinct, it became a matter of discovery where else to find this wood. From the island of Cuba a considerable quantity of the smaller sizes, of good texture and hard, suitable for small work, is obtained ; but it is from the vast forest of Mexico that the great markets of the world are now supplied, not alone with the bulk of the best mahogany, but much that is soft, though these soft grades are superior to the Baywood of olden times from Central America.

With, perhaps the exception of our oaks, no wood possesses like advantages of combined soundness, large size, durability, beauty of color and richness of figure. So, when compared with other woods, mahogany costs no more to work and stands better than any other—the only point to weigh against this last great feature is the slight difference in the first cost of the wood in the rough ; but if mahogany stands better and longer, and needs no attention afterward, surely the sole advantage of less cost at first which any other wood may possess is overcome.

But another merit, equal to any thus far mentioned, is the warmth in its color and the glory in the figure of this beautiful wood. The air of elegance, artistic effect and gentle breeding it imparts to all its surroundings, its joy and life—all these cannot be measured by a few cents a square foot. Its growing splendor with age that gives increasing satisfaction may safely be contrasted with the tameness of other woods, which, though pleasing at first, deteriorate rather than improve.   Does not mahogany add to the value of a private residence or public building?   I believe it does ; and it is this very fact that encourages so much imitation in housefinishing and in furniture.

When the real wood is used, but little more is necessary than to fill and varnish or polish, as it cannot be much improved upon. Sometimes, however, it may be deemed proper to darken it somewhat to take away the reddish hue that newly wrought mahogany presents, and this can best be done by darkening the filler, to suit the taste, trying the mixture first on a piece of the dressed stuff, until the desired shade is obtained, staining the varnish or polish with dragon's-blood or other suitable dyes, will also accomplish the desired end.

Staining by the fumes of ammonia will probably give the best results, as almost any tinge can be given the work from the newness of youth, to the mellowness of extreme age.   This method is considered the best for imparting to mahogany the appearance of age, and for those wishing to avail themselves of an easy, clean and certain means of gaining the result, fumigating offers no serious obstacle to its accomplishment; the articles necessary being easy of acquirement, and at small expense.

I give a number of receipts for making stains to imitate mahogany.   These stains may be applied to cherry, black birch, white wood, basswood, pine or sycamore, with pretty fair results. The best of these enumerated are cherry, birch and pine, as from these woods the best results are obtainable :

A good imitation of and substitute for mahogany, useful in fine manufactures, is made by procuring any species of close grained wood, such as cherry, beech or birch, and properly preparing it smooth and clean.   Then rub with diluted nitric acid, which prepares it for the materials subsequently to be applied.   These consist of one and a half ounces of dragon's-blood, dissolved in a pint of spirits of wine, and one-third of that quantity of carbonate of soda, mixed together and filtered, the liquid in this state being rubbed, or rather, laid upon the wood with a soft brush.   This process is repeated with very little alteration, and in a short interval the wood possesses all the external appearance of mahogany.

For other stains the following are given: Two ounces of dragon's blood dissolved in one quart of rectified spirits of wine, well shaken; or raw sienna in beer, with burnt sienna to give the required tone; for darker stains boil a half-pound of madder and two ounces of log-wood chips in one gallon of water and brush the decoction while hot over the wood. When dry paint with a solution of two ounces of potash in one quart of water. A solution of permanganate of potash forms a rapid and excellent brown stain.

For the color of new mahogany, see Cherry Stains.

A decoction of logwood chips, made by boiling in a closely-covered vessel one part of the chips in two parts water for two hours; then strain through a muslin cloth. Should this be required dark, as for antique mahogany, condense by a gentle heat.

Another.—For the red generally called mahogany, add to a strong decoction of logwood chips a small quantity of chloride of tin. Or add to the decoction a trifle eosine. Apply two coats.

Another.—Add to archil (orchil) sufficient eosine to produce a natural color.

Another.—Dilute alizarin-paste to the proper consistency and color.

Another.—To produce the red in oil, apply two coats of crimson or rose-lake diluted with turps and japan.

To darken mahogany, apply a weak solution of bichromate of potash in water. Apply successive coats, allowing each to dry, until the required shade is secured.

Half a pound of madder, two ounces of logwood chips boiled in a gallon of water; brush over the wood while hot. When dry, go over the whole with pearl-ash solution, two drachms to a quart of water. Size and polish. If a redder shade be required, it can be produced by smearing the surface with a strong solution permanganate of potash, which is left on for a longer or shorter time, according to the shade required; in most cases, five minutes will be enough. The wood is then carefully washed, dried and polished in the ordinary way.

The reader will understand that the mahogany stains mentioned are mostly intended for staining inferior woods to imitate mahogany, for as mentioned before only in isolated cases, will the genuine wood require to be stained— "good wine needeth no bush."—

Cherry.—(*Prunus cerasus.*)—This is a fine grained wood, tough and light, is capable of taking the very finest finish. Is harder than Baywood, and is the nearest approach in color, grain and texture, to mahogany than any other native wood.

One of the best methods for making cherry look like mahogany is to have the wood rubbed with diluted nitrc acid, which prepares it for the materials subsequently applied. Afterwards to a filtered mixture of one ounce and a half of dragon's blood dissolved in a pint of spirits of wine is added one-third that quantity of carbonate of soda. The whole constituting a very thin liquid is brushed with a soft brush over the wood. This process is repeated with very little alteration, and in a short interval of time the wood assumes the external appearance of mahogany. If the composition has been properly made the surface will resemble an artificial mirror and should this brilliancy ever decline it may be restored by rubbing the surface with a little cold drawn linseed oil.

When cherry is nicely filled and rubbed well down and not varnished, it has a soft glow not possessed by any other, and has none of those distortions of grain that are so unpleasant in mahogany. The timber is chosen from the wild cherry, which in New England and the North generally does not usually grow to a girth of more than 20 inches, but in some of the Western States and in the South frequently attains a diameter of 24 inches. The domestic fruit cherry gives some good specimens of small timber, but as the tree is rarely sacrificed until it is past bearing and is decayed, this source of supply is precarious. The facility with which cherry can be worked makes it a favorite with the cabinet-maker and the house joiner; and it also possesses the quality of "staying where it is put," and that is more than can be said of many of the hard woods.

I give below several stains for making pine and other suitable woods to have an appearance of cherry.

1. To prepare this color in water stain, boil in a gallon of water one pound of Spanish annotto and one ounce of concentrated lye (potash). Should this not be deep enough, allow the water to evaporate by a gentle heat. The stain can also be darkened by adding gamboge previously dissolved in a weak potash solution.

2. Gamboge in oil, diluted with turpentine, and a little japan added as a siccative. This produces the same color in oil as the former in water stain, and can be deepened with dragon's blood in oil or finely-ground burnt sienna in oil.

3. Mix together, by stirring, 1 quart of spirits of turpentine, 1 pint of varnish, and 1 lb. of dry burnt sienna; apply with a brush and after it has been on about five minutes wipe it off with rags. This stain takes about 12 hours to dry.

4. Take 1 quart alcohol, 2 ozs. of dragon's blood; pulverize the latter along with ¼ oz. of alkanet root; mix and let stand in a warm place a couple of days. Shake frequently in the meantime. Apply with a sponge or brush. Two or three coats may be required. This makes a fine stain.

There are a number of other compounds, but it is considered that the above are ample for all ordinary purposes. When stains are wanted in large quantities it is much better to purchase them, as a number of excellent mixtures are now obtainable, among which may be mentioned those of the Chilton Mfg. Co., New York, who make fine ebony, mahogany and cherry stains. Aniline stain may be purchased at any color shop.

Ash (*Fraxinus excelsior.*) This wood is now used very much by cabinet makers and house joiners in place of oak, and I have often seen furniture palmed off, to unsuspecting customers as antique oak and in one instance I know of an architect who specified oak, and who "passed" a mixture of white and black ash, as oak, either knowingly or otherwise. I am not sure that the owners in either case lost anything, for good sound Canadian ash, is decidedly better than dosey red oak.

In finishing ash, either black or white, the same methods are adopted as for finishing oak and similar processes will give similar results. Ingenious stainers and finishes can make ash resemble oak wainscot, in vein and color so correctly that it is almost impossible for the most experienced connoisseur to distinguish the genuine from the spurious. - In order to do this some finishers make a commencement by sketching out, upon certain parts of the ash exterior, the requisite white veins, by means of a camelhair pencil, with white stain ; that done, they coat the veins with thin varnish, and then darken the general ground, dealing carefully throughout the entire process with the veined portions. Others stain and embody, *i. e.* French polish—the ash with the ordinary preparation, after which they pursue an operative course termed "champing" ; that is, scratching fancifully, so as to form the veins, upon different parts of the coated surface, before it gets time to harden, with a saturated rag. The former process is, however, the most suitable of the two.

Birch. (*Betula Nigra.*) or Canadian birch is superior to all other birches for constructive purposes and when properly finished has a fine quiet refined look that commands itself to all lovers of domestic woods. So popular has the use of black birch become within the last ten years, that the price of good grades has advanced from $8 per M feet, in 1880 to $100 per M feet, in 1892.

Black birch is a close-grained, handsome wood, and can be easily stained to resemble walnut exactly. It is just as easy to work, and is suitable for nearly, if not all, the purposes to which walnut is at present applied. Birch is much the same color as cherry, but the latter wood is now scarce, and consequently dear. When properly stained it is almost impossible to distinguish the difference between it and walnut, as it is susceptible of a beautiful polish, equal to any wood now used in the manufacture of furniture, and inside finishings.

There is a species of bird's-eye birch, but it is very scarce. An evidence of the weight and solidity of the wood is the fact that it will sink after being a few days on the water. It also possesses the quality of durability in a pre-eminent degree.

Birch is generally finished the same as cherry, and directions given under that head will apply here also.

Pine.—(*Pinus Strobus*). If oak is the king of woods, pine is most assuredly " president," for it is at once the most useful and the most democratic of woods. It is found in the halls of the great and powerful, and in the cottage of the most humble among us. It is strong and vigorous, plain or ornamental and is not out of place either in the backwoodsman's cabin or in the stately cathedral, and like a true man of the world, it adapts itself to every condition that circumstances may place it in.

Pine can be made to look like any known wood, but is at its best when left natural and finished in clear shellac. There is no wood grows, that will convey so cheerful a feeling to the beholder as yellow or white pine finished in a natural state. Next to being finished in a natural state, is to imitate mahogany or light cherry which coloring it takes readily.

Where the pine—of any kind—is to be either stained or left natural, it should be " quarter sawed" as it will show a finer grain, shrink less, and last longer. The softness of its texture and its susceptibility to injury may have had some influence in preventing its general use for ornamental purposes, but the wood can be "filled," so that much of this objection is removed. Its pure white color—white as compared with other woods—recommends it for purposes for which holly has been heretofore used; and the size of the timber from which clear boards may be cut is greatly in its favor, boards of a width of sixteen, and even twenty inches being not uncommon, with no shade of distinction between sap wood and heart, and only the faintest perceptible grain.

Some specimens lately examined show a greatly enhanced beauty by very simple treatment—the filling with warm shellac varnish, bleached shellac in alcohol, applied with a brush while warm. Several coats are given, the last coat being rubbed with pumice and rotton stone, moistened with water, not oil. A finish of a flowing coat of copal varnish completes the preparation. Thus treated, the wood is of a faint creamy tint, with an appearance of semi-transparency. Beautiful gradations of tone were obtained by panels of this prepared pine.

Most of the stains given under previous heads, are applicable to pine, I add, however a few more, so that the workmen may have a number of recipes to draw from :

For Walnut No. 1.—Dissolve by boiling one part each of Epson salt and permanganate of potash in about twenty-five parts of water. This stain may be improved by adding a little eosine, and it works best when applied hot.

2. Catechu broken into crumbs and boiled in about twice its bulk of water until dissolved. To darken to the required depth, add bichromate of potash previously dissolved in about eight times its equivalent of water. If the deep yellok shade peculiar to the Southern walnut be required, add yellow chromate of potash. For the reddish shade of the Northern wood, add more eosine.

3. For oil stain, use Vandyke brown toned up with the siennas, the colors being strictly pure and finely ground in oil, and diluted with turpentine and a small amount of japan.

4. Burnt Turkey umber mixed in the same way as the former.

5. Mix together, by stirring, 1 quart spirits of turpentine, 1 pint asphaltum varnish, 1 pint of japan, 1 lb. dry burnt umber, 1 lb. dry Venetian red ; apply with a brush. This stain is transparent, and allows the grain of the wood to show through.

6. Boil 1½ ounces washing soda, and ¼ ounce bichromate of potash, in 1 quart of water; add 2½ ounces Vandyke brown. This stain may be used either hot or cold.

7. With a brush apply a thin solution of permanganate of

potassa in water, until the desired color is produced, allowing each coat to dry before another is applied.

For Mahogany or Cherry No. 1. For mahogany, use a pint of turpentine and an ounce of color known as dragon's blood. Dissolve and shake well before applying. For ebony, use hot liquor from logwood chips, and after dry apply a coat of tincture of steel. For walnut, use two ounces of washing soda, darkened with Vandyke brown in water. Add two ounces of bichromate of potash in pint and a half of water.

2. Mix together, by stirring, 1 quart of spirits of turpentine, 1 pint of varnish, and 1 lb. of dry burnt sienna ; apply with a brush, and after it has been on about five minutes wipe it off with rags. This stain takes about 12 hours to dry.

3. Take 1 quart alcohol, 2 ozs. of dragon's-blood ; pulverize the latter along with $\frac{1}{4}$ oz. of alkanet root ; mix, and let stand in a warm place a couple of days. Shake frequently in the meantime. Apply with a sponge or brush. Two or three coats may be required. This makes a fine stain.

For Rosewood No. 1. Mix in a bottle $\frac{1}{4}$ lb. of extract of logwood, 1 oz. salts of tartar, and 1 pint of water ; in another bottle, put 1 lb. of old iron in small pieces, and 1 pint of vinegar, which, after standing twenty-four hours, will be ready for use ; make a hard stiff brush with a piece of rattan sharpened at one end in a wedge shape, pounding it so as to separate the fibre. Mix in 1 pint of varnish, $\frac{1}{4}$ lb. of finely-powdered rose-pink. The materials are now ready, and the first thing in the process is to stain the wood with the logwood stain ; give two coats of this, allowing the first to become nearly dry before applying the second; then dip the rattan brush in the vinegar, and with it form the grain, after which give the work a coat of the varnish and rose pink. There can be no definite directions given for graining, except to study the natural wood and imitate it as near as possible. With the above materials skilfully applied, any common wood can be made to resemble rosewood so nearly that it will take a good judge to distinguish the difference.

2. Boil 1 lb. of logwood in 1 gallon of water, add a double handful of walnut shell, boil the whole again, strain the liquor and add to it 1 pint of the best vinegar. It is then ready for use. Apply it boiling hot, and when the wood is dry, form red veins in imitation of the grain of rosewood with a brush dipped in the following solution : Nitric acid, 1 pint ; metallic tin, 1 oz.; sal ammoniac, 1 oz. Mix and set aside to dissolve, occasionally shaking. If carefully executed it will give the appearance of dark rosewood.

For surface stains the following are sometimes used : The colors are all to be mixed with very thin glue size, laid on warm with a soft woollen material, and the wood wiped dry after application. All the colors used is staining should be well pulverized, and before use the liquid should be strained.

Imitation Oak Stain.—Equal parts burnt umber and brown ochre.

Imitation Mahogany Stain.—One part Venetian red, and two parts yellow lead.

Imitation Rosewood Stain.—Venetian red, darkened with lamp black to required shade.

Imitation Walnut Stain.—Burnt umber and yellow ochre, mixed in proportions to give desired shade.

Before leaving the subject of pine, it may be as well to say a few words regarding the long leaved, or Georgia pine (*Pinus Pulustris.*) as a great deal of it is used now in and about the city of New York, and other large centres. This wood is very fine, strong and lasting. Some of it is insusceptible of fine finish, but the best success with it, is when treated with shellac finish. In all other respects, when used as a finishing material, it may be treated the same as ordinary pine.

Walnut.—(*Juglans Nigra.*)—As this wood is seldom or never stained it is unnecessary to say more about it other than it may be treated like oak cherry or birch. It looks well filled and finished in shellac. Birch stained and properly finished looks very much like walnut, and with a little care in getting a proper tint in the stain, can scarcely be known from the real thing. "Filling," in walnut finishing, is one of the most important processes, if the richness of the wood is desired to be shown as much depends on the "tint" as on the filling material.

Poplar.—(*Populus balsamifera*).

Basswood.—(*Tieia Americana.*)

Cedar.—White—(*cupressus thuyoides*) which is really a spruce, and all similar woods, should never be finished in a natural state. Deep stains or surface stains should always be employed on these woods if they are not to be painted.

Beech.—(*Fagus ferruginea*) This is one of the unnoticed woods of former years but is now gradually gaining in favor as a decorative wood. It is cheap and also quite abundant, while the more popular hard woods are beginning to grow scarcer and higher in price. Beechwood has a fine grain, is quite durable, and can be used in the manufacture of furniture and for decorative purposes generally. The red variety has a handsome appearance and is especially suitable for use where a good imitation of cherry is desired.

If " quarter sawed " it shows a fine grain and has a character distinctly its own which I think has never been properly appreciated. When quartered, properly finished, filled and polished, it looks something like dark leopard wood. It will assume a dark mahogany color if prepared like cherry or birch, or it may be made to appear like walnut if treated with walnut stains and finish.

Elm.—(*Ulmus Americana.*)

Chestnut.—(*castanea vesca.*)

Butternut.—(*Juglans cinerea.*)

These three woods are often used in inferior work, and are very soft and and easily dented. The best is perhaps the elm, which does very well for bath-room finish, panels for ash doors and similar work. All require a great deal of " filling " and this should be well rubbed in if a good job is required. All of these woods have a very coarse grain, but if care is taken in selecting the material, very odd and oftimes pleasing effects may be obtained.   Any of the stains used on pine, will answer for these woods, dependent of course on the tints desired.   The best results with these woods is derived by giving the work one coat of shellac after filling and staining, then sandpaper well and apply your varnish or oil finish or whatever you purpose finishing in.

Cypress.—(*Cupressus sempervierens.*) The light the dark and the bald are good woods and are coming more and more in favor every day.

This wood contains a very small amount of resin, and a very high polish can be given it ; in fact, because of its not being affected by moisture, it is being used for cisterns, hogsheads, and sugar, molasses and honey barrels.   The red cypress is the favorite, and some of it is so heavy that it will sink upon being placed in water.   The white variety in much lighter, and will float after being deadened a short while before being cut, but it has not the firm grain of the red.   The red cypress has a straight trunk with a small top, and the bark when cut has a reddish tint.   These woods may be treated like cherry or brich with good results. They look well when left their natural color and finished '' dead finish.''

Sycamore. or Buttonwood, as it is sometimes called (*acer pseudo platanus*) when quarter sawed and properly finished makes a good appearance, and in many cases is superceding cherry owing to its beauty and cheapness.   Heretofore its natural beauty has been destroyed in many cases by staining the wood, and thus preventing the development of many chemical changes which take place and are thrown to the surface when properly treated.   When quarter sawed, a light bodied and light colored shellac should be used, when by a natural chemical process a beautiful silver leaf is developed and the surface assumes a charming pink hue.

Hemlock.—(*Abies Canadensis.*) This is rarely used for finishing owing to its brittleness and splintery nature.   Clean boards, however, made into panels or other similar work and then finished in natural color, assumes a very handsome appearance.   It has a a pink tint of the most delicate kind which improves and mellows with age. It should be finished in the same manner as pine.

Rosewood.—(*Dalbergia Nigra.*) It seldom falls to the lot of the ordinary finisher to have to " try his hand " on the genuine wood, but sometimes it *does happen* and it is just as well that he should be armed with the means to wrestle with the work if such is ever thrown in his way. To finish rosewood, requires about the same treatment as mahogany, though, as a matter of fact, many pieces of rosewood will be found to have a coarser grain than mahogany, and will require much care in filling. The main thing to be observed, is to see that the filling is a shade or two darker than the wood to be filled, before any varnish is laid on. For imitation of rosewood I give below a few recipes:

Take half a pound of logwood, boil it with three pints of water till it is of a very dark red, to which add about half an ounce of salt of tartar. When boiling hot, stain your wood with two or three coats, taking care that it is nearly dry between each; then, with a stiff, flat brush, such as is used for graining, make streaks with a very deep black stain, which if carefully executed will be very near the appearance of dark rosewood. The following is another method: Stain your wood all over with a black stain, and when dry, with a brush as above dipped in the bright liquid form real veins in imitation of the grain of rosewood, which will produce, when well managed, a beautiful effect. A handy brush for the purpose of graining may be made by taking a flat brush such as used for varnishing, and cuttting the sharp points of the hairs and making the edge irregular; by cutting out a few hairs here and there the grain may be imitated with great accuracy.

This is suitable to pine, cedar, cyprus, whitewood, basswoods while the following should only be used in mahogany, cherry, or birch, spread on the surface of the material a concentrated solution of hypermagnate of potassa, to act until the desired shade is obtained. Five minutes suffice, ordinarily, to give a deep color, a few trials indicating the proper proportions. The hypermagnate of potassa is decomposed by the vegetable fibre with the precipitation of brown peroxide of maganese, which the influence of the potassa, at the same time set free, fixes in a durable manner the fibres. When the action is terminated the wood is carefully washed with water, dried, and then oiled and polished in the usual manner. The effect produced by this process in several woods is really remarkable.

It has been a mystery to many people why the dark wood so highly prized for furniture is called " Rosewood." Its color certainly does not look much like a rose, so we must look for some other reason. It is claimed by some that when the tree is first cut the wood possesses a very strong roselike fragrance, hence the name. This is the most probable reason for its name. There are about a half a dozen kinds of rosewood trees. The varieties are found in South America, and in the East Indies and neighboring islands. Sometimes the trees grow so large that boards or planks four feet broad and ten feet in length can be cut from them. The broad boards are used for the tops of piano fortes. When growing in the forests the tree is remarkable for its beauty, but such its value in manufacturing as an ornamental wood that some of the forests where it once grew abundantly now have scarcely a single specimen left.

I have purposely left unmentioned a number of our finest woods such as our maples, and others, which, would it not increase the size of this volume, beyond reasonable dimensions. I should have more to say concerning them. The workmen will know, from what has already been said, how these light woods may be treated, and I may add, that the various maples, though rather light in color for general purposes, make the most delicate of finish. Gum wood of late, has been used to some extent and is not hard to deal with when to be finished. It should be treated about as cherry and birch, and finished in a similar way, and when done nicely the work looks quite well.

Redwood is getting to be a favorite wood with some builders, owing no doubt to its cheapness, and its easiness to work. It may be classed among the softer woods and requires treating about the same as chestnut, butternut and the cedars. The following formula and directions have been highly recommended as a finish, but for my own part, I prefer using Wheeler's filler as I think better results are obtained. Here is the formula:

Take one quart Spirits Tupentine.

Add one pound Corn Starch.

Add ¼ " Burnt Sienna.

Add one tablespoonful Raw Linseed Oil.

Add " " Brown Japan.

Mix thoroughly, apply with a brush, let it stand say fifteen minutes; rub off all you can with fine shavings or a soft rag, then let it stand *at least twenty-four hours* that it may sink into and *harden* the fibres of the wood, afterward apply two coats of white shellac; rub down well with fine flint paper, then put on from two to five coats best polishing varnish ; after it is well dried rub with water and pumice-stone ground very fine, stand a day to dry ; after being washed clean with chamois, rub with water and rotten-stone ; dry, wash as before clean, and rub with olive oil until dry.

Some use cork for sand-papering and polishing, but a smooth block of hard wood like maple is better. When treated in this way redwood will be found the peer of any wood for real beauty and life as a house trim or finish. By proper attention, redwood may be made to appear like mahogany or cherry but its softness is very much against it.

General Recipes.—*Ebonizing.*—Prepare some shellac varnish by dissolving half a pound of gum shellac in a quart of alcohol ; put in a tightly corked bottle, set in a warm place, and shake frequently. When completely dissolved, add sufficient dry lamp or bone black. It will require only about a heaping tablespoonful to half a pint of varnish. Should it be too thick to flow easily from the brush, and spread evenly, add alcohol. Give the wood two or three coats of this, which can be done within two days. For fine work give three coats of the black varnish and allow it to dry thoroughly ; then take some oo or ooo sand-paper and rub the work down lightly until the surface is smooth and even, being careful not to rub through to the wood.   Then apply two or three coats more, and rub down again with the sandpaper; give two coats more and allow it to dry perfectly hard.   Make some rubbers of felt, an old felt hat is good, by tacking the felt on blocks of soft wood of proper shape, which should be flat, concave or convex to fit the work.   Apply a few drops of sewing machine oil to the felt and sprinkle on a pinch of pulverized pumice stone.   Rub the work with this, keeping the rubber moist with oil and supplied with the pumice, until the wood shows a perfectly smooth surface, without any gloss.   When it has all been gone over wipe off the surface and rub clean with dry flannel cloths.   The result is fine imitation of ebony.   If the shellac varnish is colored with aniline instead of lamp-black, the finished surface is smoother and finer.

Others.—1. infuse gall-nut in vinegar, into which rusty nails have been soaked ; paint the wood with this, polish and burnish when dry.   2. Wash the wood repeatedly with a solution of sul-phate of iron, made by dissolving 2 oz. of sulphate in a pint of hot water.   When dry, apply a hot decoction of logwood and nut-galls two or three times.   When dry, clean with a wet sponge and then polish.   3.   Brush the wood with a strong decoction of logwood chips several times.   When dry, give it a coat of vinegar in which rusty iron has been placed.   Dissolve beeswax in turpentine by setting in a warm place; apply warm with a brush, and rub it till it shines.   4.   Wash with a concentrated aqueous solution of logwood several times, and then with a solu-tion of acetate of iron of 40 deg. Baume.   Repeat till a deep black is produced.   5.   Put 2 oz. of logwood chips with 1¼ oz. of copperas in a quart of water, boil, and lay on hot.   When dry, wet the surface again with 2 oz. of steel filings dissolved in half a pint of vinegar.   When dry again, sand-paper smooth, then oil, then fill it with powdered drop-black mixed in the filler.   Work to be ebonized should be smooth and free from holes.   Give it a light coat of quick drying varnish, then rub with finely pulverized pumice stone and linseed oil until very smooth. 6. Boil ½ pound of chip logwood in two quarts of water, and add ½ oz. of verdigris and ½ oz. of copperas, strain, and put in ½ pound of rusty steel filings. With this go over the work a second time. 7. A pound of logwood boiled in four quarts of water, add two handfuls of walnut shells or peel, boil up again, take out the chips, add a pint of vinegar, and apply boiling. Afterwards dissolve 1 oz. of green copperas in a quart of boiling water and apply hot. 8. First sponge the wood with a solution of chlorhydrate of aniline in water, to which a small quantity of copper chloride is added. When dry, go over again with a solution of potassium bichromate. Repeat this twice or thrice. 9. One gallon of vinegar, ½ pound of green copperas, ¼ pound of China blue, 2 oz. nut-gall, 2 pounds extract of logwood. Boil all these over a slow fire, and add half a pint of iron-rust. Apply as usual. A good varnish for ebonized work is made by dissolving in alcohol some black wax.

Stains.—Many excellent stains for pine may be obtained by using the ordinary graining colors, Vandyke brown, raw and burnt sienna, ultramarine blue, etc., applied with a brush, without previous preparation and then wiped off with a cloth—a method that brings out clearly the grain or marks of the wood, which in pitch pine, now being extensively used for fittings, are often extremely beautiful. A better method for general work, French polish being ordinarily too expensive, is, where dark oak or mahogany stains are not wanted, light varnishes, of which two coats are to be applied. The glue size with which the work is first coated, in order to fill up the pores of the wood, should not be too thick, as in that case it is liable to crack.

Logwood, lime, brown soft-soap, dyed oil, sulphate of iron, nitrate of silver exposed to the sun's rays, carbonate of soda, bichromate and permanganate of potash, and other alkaline preparations, are used for darkening the wood; the last three are specially recommended. The solution is applied by dissolving one ounce of the alkali in two gills of boiling water, diluted to the required tone. The surface is saturated with a sponge or flannel, and immediately dried with soft rags. The carbonate is used for dark woods. Oil tinged with rose madder may be applied to hard woods like birch, and a red oil is prepared from soaked alkanet root in linseed oil. The grain of yellow pine can be brought out by two or three coats of japan, much diluted with turpentine, and afterwards oiled and rubbed. To give mahogany the appearance of age, lime water used before oiling is a good plan. In staining wood, the best and most transparent effect is obtained by repeated light coats of the same. For oak stain a strong solution of oxalic acid is employed ; for mahogany, dilute nitric acid. A primary coat or a coat of wood fillers is advantageous. For mahogany stains, the following are given: two ounces of dragon's-blood dissolved in one quart of rectified spirits of wine, well shaken, or raw sienna in beer, with burnt sienna to give the required tone ; for darker stains boil half pound of madder and two ounces of logwood chips in one gallon of water, and brush the decoction while hot over the wood ; when dry, paint with a solution of two ounces of potash in one quart of water. A solution of permangate of potash forms a rapid and excellent brown stain.

Oak or ash may be stained brown by using linseed oil and benzine half and half, and burnt umber or Vandyke brown incorporated with this. Maple can be stained green-gray by using copperas in water; oak will also be changed to a dark green blue through the same agency, the effect on ash being various shades of olive green. Ammonia applied to oak produces the bronze olive tint now used so much by architects.

Wash any compact wood with a boiling decoction of logwood three or four times, allowing it to dry between each application. Then wash it with a solution of acetate of iron, which is made by dissolving iron fillings in vinegar. This stain is very black, and penetrates to a considerable depth into the wood, so that ordinary scratching or chipping does not show the original color.

A wash of one part of nitric acid in ten parts of water will, if well done, impart a stain resembling mahogany to pine wood which does not contain much resin. When the wood is thoroughly dry, shellac varnish will impart a fine finish to the surface. A glaze of carmine or lake will produce a rosewood finish. A turpentine extract of alkanet root produces a beautiful stain which admits of French polishing. Asphaltum, thinned with turpentine, makes an excellent mahogany color on new wood.

A Method.—Of imparting to any plain white wood the appearance of cedar wood is as follows :—Mix two parts of catechu, and one part of caustic soda, in a hundred parts of water (all by weight). The article to be stained should be boiled in this solution for some hours, and is then rinsed in clear water and dried. If the desired depth of tone has not been obtained, a second boiling must be resorted to. This stain is said to sink so deep into the wood that even thick sheets of veneer thus treated will be colored right through ; while other wood articles thus stained may be safely manipulated without any fear of the original color of the wood showing through.

For a Brown Stain.—Boil 1 lb. of the brown pigment called Terre de Cassel with 4 quarts of water, until it is reduced one-third. Mix two ounces (Troy) of white potash with sufficient water to dissolve it, and mix with the Terre de Cassel. This stain must be applied with a brush, two or even three times, according to the depth of the shade required.

Another.—Paint the wood with a solution made by boiling one pot of catechu with thirty parts of water and a little soda ; when dry paint over with another solution made of one part bichromate of potash and thirty parts water. By a little difference in the mode of treatment, and by varying the strength of the solutions, several shades of color may be given.

For a Black Dye.—Put 6 lbs. of chip logwood into the copper, with as many veneers as it will conveniently hold, without pressing too tight ; fill it with water, and let it boil *slowly* for about three hours ; then add half a pound of powdered verdigris, half a pound of copperas, and four ounces of bruised nut-galls ; fill the copper up with vinegar as the water evaporates ; let it boil gently two hours each day till the wood is dyed through.

To Brighten Stains.—Any of the stains named (except the surface stains) will be rendered much more brilliant by an application of the following : 1 oz. nitric acid, ½ teaspoonful muriatic acid, ¼ oz. grain tin, 2 ozs. rain water. Mix in a bottle, at least two days before using, and keep the bottle well corked.

The above stains are probably the most important to a house finisher, and, as they have all been employed and found practicable, they can be relied upon. In performing a small job it will generally be found more convenient and economical to obtain the stain from some furniture shop where it is kept in bulk.

The best way to preserve stain is to keep it in bottles or jugs. It is said that four or five drops of creosote added to a quart of stain will prevent it from becoming mouldy and stagnant.

The stainers at the furniture shops have contrived a scheme to prevent their hands from becoming deeply stained while at work, by dipping them into a quick-dry varnish or oil shellac, and then in cleansing them they rinse them first in water to remove the stain, and then submit them to a turpentine bath, thus removing the varnish.

Miscellaneous.—Many processes have of late been applied to the finishing of woodwork, such as staining in various colors, fumigating and other methods. A new finish is now practised in the European market, and is known as the Rubenick process. It is used for giving a metallic surface to wood, and consists in first immersing the wood in a bath of caustic alkaline lye, in which it is allowed to remain for two or three days, according to the degree of permeability of the wood, at a temperature of 167° to 194° F. From this bath the wood passes to another of hydro-sulphate of calcium, to which is added, after 24 or 36 hours, a concentrated solution of sulphur. Here it remains for about 48 hours at a temperature of 95° to 122° F., and, lastly, for from 30 to 50 hours the wood is immersed in a solution of acetate of lead at the same temperature. The timber, thus pickled, is allowed to dry, when it is said to be susceptible, after burnishing, of a high polish and even metallic luster, which is more brilliant if the surfaces of the wood have been previously rubbed with lead, tin or zinc plates, and then polished with a glass or porcelain burnisher. Treated in this way the wood may assume the appearance of a metallic mirror, being also hard and very strong.

With the majority of lumbermen the term hardwood includes everything except white pine, and is accepted in that sense generally by the trade, though in reality there are two or three woods, such as buckeye and Southern white lynn, that are softer than white pine. Some writer, we know not who, says : "The relative hardness of woods is calculated by the hickory, which is the toughest. Estimating this at 100, we get for pignut hickory 96, white oak 84, white ash 77, dogwood 75, scrub oak 73, white hazel, 72, apple tree 70, red oak 79, white beech 65, black walnut 65, black birch 62, yellow and black oak, 60, hard maple 56, white elm 58, red cedar 56, cherry 55, yellow pine 54, chestnut 52, yellow poplar 51, butternut and white birch 43, and white pine 35. "

According to this formula, woods possessing a degree of hardness equal to only about 40 per cent., or less than that of hickory, should not be classed as hardwoods. Such woods are, however, limited in quantity, and are not of sufficient importance to justify a classification, and the trade will continue to construe hardwood to mean everything except white pine.

Dyeing wood is mostly applied for the purpose of veneers, while staining is more generally had recourse to give the desired color to the article after it has been manufactured. In the one case, the color should penetrate throughout, while in the latter the surface is all that is essential.

In dyeing, pear tree, holly and beech, take the best black ; but for most colors holly is preferable. It is also best to have wood as young and as newly cut as possible. After the veneers are cut, they should be allowed to lie in a trough of water for four or five

days before they are put into the copper ; as the water, acting as
a purgative to the wood, brings out an abundance of slimy matter,
which must be removed, or the wood will never be a good color.
After this purificatory process, they should be dried in the open
air for at least twelve hours.   They are then ready for the copper.   By these simple means the color will strike much quicker,
and be of a brighter hue.   It would also add to the improvement
of the colors, if, after the veneers have boiled a few bours, they
are taken out, dried in the air, and again immersed in the coloring copper.   Always dry veneers in the open air, for fire invari-
ably injures the colors.

Fine Black Dye.—Put 6 lbs. of chip logwood into the copper,
with as many veneers as it will conveniently hold, without pressing too tight ; fill it with water, and let it boil *slowly* for about
three hours ; then add half a pound of powdered verdigris, half
a pound of copperas, and 4 ounces of bruised nut-galls ; fill the
copper up with vinegar as the water evaporates ; let it boil gently
two hours each day till the wood is dyed through.

Another.—Procure some liquor from a tanner's pit, or make a
decoction of oak bark, and to every gallon of the liquor add a
quarter of a pound of green copperas, and mix them well together ; put the liquor into the copper, and make it quite hot, but
not boil ; immerse the veneers in it, and let them remain for an
hour ; take them out, and expose them to the air, till it has penetrated its substance ;   then add some logwood to the solution,
place the veneers again in it, and let it simmer for two or three
hours; let the whole cool gradually, dry the veneers in the shade,
and they will be a very fine black.

Fine Blue Dye.—Into a clean glass bottle put 1 lb. of oil of vitriol, and 4 ozs. of the best indigo pounded in a mortar (take care
to set the bottle in a basin or earthen glazed pan, as it will fer-
ment); then put the veneers into a copper or stone trough; fill it
rather more than one-third with water, and add as much of the
vitriol and indigo (stirring it about) as will make a fine blue, which

may be known by trying it with a piece of white paper or wood, Let the veneers remain till the dye has struck through.

The color will be much improved if the solution of indigo in vitriol be kept a few weeks before using it. The color will strike better if the veneers are boiled in plain water till completely soaked through, and then allowed for a few hours to dry partially, previous to being immersed in the dye.

Another—Throw pieces of quicklime into soft water; stir it well; when settled, strain or pour off the clear part; then to every gallon add ten or twelve ounces of the best turnsole; put the whole into the copper with the veneers, which should be of white holly, and prepared as usual by boiling in water; let them simmer gently till the color has sufficiently penetrated, but be careful not to let them boil in it, as it would injure the color.

A Fine Yellow Dye.—Reduce 4 lbs. of the root of barberry, by sawing, to dust, which put in a copper or brass trough; add 4 ozs. of turmeric and 4 gallons of water, then put in as many white holly veneers as the liquor will cover; boil them together for three hours, often turning them; when cool, add 2 ozs. of aquafortis and the dye will strike through much sooner.

A Bright Yellow Dye.—To every gallon of water necessary to cover the veneers, add 1 lb. of French berries; boil the veneers till the color has penetrated through; add to the infusion of the French berries, the liquid for brightening colors given on page 78, and let the veneers remain for two or three hours, and the color will be very bright.

Bright Green Dye.—Proceed as in either of the previous receipts to produce a yellow; but instead of adding aquafortis or the brightening liquid, add as much vitriolated indigo (see page 80) as will produce the desired color.

Green Dye.—Dissolve 4 ozs. of the best verdigris, and of sap-green and indigo half an ounce each in 3 pints of the best vinegar; put in the veneers, and gently boil till the color has penetrated sufficiently.

The hue of the green may be varied by altering the proportion

6

of the ingredients; and it is advised, unless wanted for a particular purpose, to leave out the sap-green, as it is a vegetable color very apt to change, or turn brown, when exposed to the air.

Bright Red Dye.—To 2 lbs. of genuine Brazil dust, add 4 gallons of water; put in as many veneers as the liquor will cover; boil them for three hours; then add 2 ozs. of alum, and 2 ozs. of aquafortis, and keep it lukewarm until it has struck through.

Red Dye.—To every pound of logwood chips, add 2 gallons of water; put in the veneers, and boil as in the last; then add a sufficient quantity of the brightening liquid (see page 78) till you see the color to your mind; keep the whole as warm as the finger can be borne in it, till the color has sufficiently penetrated.

The logwood chips should be picked from all foreign substances, with which it generally abounds, as bark, dirt, etc.; and it is always best when fresh cut, which may be known by its appearing of a bright-red color; for if stale, it will look brown, and not yield so much coloring matter.

Purple Dve.—To 2 lbs. of chip logwood and half a pound of Brazil dust, add 4 gallons of water, and after putting in the veneers, boil them for at least three hours; then add 6 ozs. of pearlash and 2 ozs. of alum; let them boil for two or three hours every day, till the color has struck through.

The Brazil dust only contributes to make the purple of a more red cast; you may, therefore, omit it, if you require a deep bluish purple.

Another.—Boil 2 lbs. of logwood, either in chips or powder, in 4 gallons of water, with the veneers; after boiling till the color is well struck in, add by degrees vitriolated indigo (see page 80) till the purple is of the shade required, which may be known by trying it with a piece of paper; let it then boil for one hour, and keep the liquid in a milk-warm state till the color has penetrated the veneer. This method, when properly managed, will produce a brilliant purple, not so likely to fade as the foregoing.

Liquid For Brightening AND SETTING COLORS.—To every pint of strong aquafortis, add 1 oz. of grain tin, and a piece of

sal-ammoniac of the size of a walnut; set it by to dissolve, shake
the bottle round with the cork out, from time to time; in the
course of two or three days it will be fit for use. This will be
found an admirable liquid to add to any color, as it not only
brightens it, but renders it less likely to fade from exposure to the
air.

Orange Dye.—Let the veneers be dyed by either of the methods
given in page 81, of a fine deep yellow, and while they are still
wet and saturated with the dye, transfer them to the bright red
dye as in page 82, till the color penetrates equally throughout.

Silver Grey Dye.—Expose to the weather in a cast-iron pot
of six or eight gallons, old iron nails, hoops, etc., till covered
with rust; add 1 gallon of vinegar and 2 of water, boil all well
for an hour; have the veneers ready, which must be hard-wood
(not too dry,)put them in the copper used to dye black, and pour
the iron liquor over them; add 1 lb. of chip logwood and 2 ozs.
of bruised nut-galls; then boil up another pot of the iron liquor
to supply the copper with, keeping the veneers covered, and boiling two hours a day, till the required color is obtained.

Gray Dye.—Expose any quantity of old iron, or what is better,
the borings of gun-barrels, etc., in any convenient vessel, and
from time to time sprinkle them with spirits of salt (muriatic acid)
diluted in four times its quantity of water, till they are very
thickly covered with rust; then to every six pounds add a gallon
of water, in which has been dissolved two ounces of salt of tartar;
lay the veneers in the copper, and cover them with this liquid;
let it boil for two or three hours till well soaked, then to every
gallon of liquor add a quarter of a pound of green copperas, and
keep the whole at a moderate temperature till the dye has sufficiently penetrated.

Gilding, Silvering and Bronzing are processes of applying to
previously prepared surfaces a thin layer of gold or silver leaf, or
in bronzing, of a fine powder, prepared from various metals and
intended to imitate the peculiar appearance of genuine bronze.

The processes of gilding and silvering being identical, the description of one will suffice to explain the other.

Gilding.—Gold leaf, applied to articles of furniture as a means of decoration, is used in two ways; it is applied over an ordinary varnish or other finish, in which case but little special preparation is necessary; or, as when used for picture frames, cornices, etc., it is appled to a specially prepared foundation, the basis of which is whiting, mixed with various other ingredients suggested by experience or fancy. In either case, the gold leaf is caused to adhere to the work, by size specially prepared for the purpose, receipts for which follow herewith; the size being first applied to the work, and when it has become of the right consistency, the gold is laid upon it. OIL-GILDING and BURNISH-GILDING are different methods used to obtain certain desired effects, the former principally for articles exposed to the weather, and for heightening the effect of incised carving or engraving, and the latter for picture-frames and articles having a specially prepared foundation, whose entire surface is to be gilded. It is intended that the gold shall adhere to the work only in the places to which the size has been applied, but the smallest portion of oil or even a slight dampness may cause the gold to partially adhere to the adjoining surface, resulting in slightly ragged edges; to prevent this, before applying the size to the desired design, the entire surface is covered with a thin film of some substance perfectly free from moisture, and easily removable by water, after completion of the process.

The Requisites.—First, a sufficient quantity of leaf-gold, which is of two sorts—the deep gold, as it is called, and the pale gold. The former is the best; the latter very useful, and may occasionally be introduced for variety or effect.

Second, a gilder's cushion: an oblong piece of wood, covered with rough calf-skin, stuffed with flannel several times doubled, with a border of parchment, about four inches deep, at one end, to prevent the air blowing the leaves about when placed on the cushion.

Thirdly, a gilding-knife, with a straight and very smooth edge, to cut the gold.

Fourthly, several camel-hair pencils in sizes, and tips, made of a few long camel's hairs put between two cards, in the same manner as hairs are put into tin cases for brushes, thus making a flat brush with a very few hairs.

Lastly, a burnisher, which is a crooked piece of agate set in a long wooden handle.

Sizes.—These are of two kinds: oil sizes are those which when applied, present an adhesive surface, requiring the immediate laying of the gold-leaf upon it ; of this class is the oil-size commonly used in decorating furniture ; water-sizes are those that are allowed to become dry and hard when applied, and are rendered adhesive when the gold is to be laid, by brushing over with water ; for burnish-gilding these are always employed, as oil-size does not dry sufficiently hard to permit of burnishing.

Oil Size for Oil-Gilding.—Grind calcined red-ochre with the best and oldest drying-oil. When desired for use, add sufficient oil of turpentine to make it work freely.

Parchment-Size.—For preparing Frames, etc.—To half a pound of parchment shavings, or cuttings of white leather, add three quarts of water, and boil it in a proper vessel till reduced to nearly half the quantity ; then take it off the fire, and strain it through a sieve. Be careful in the boiling to keep it well stirred, and do not let burn.

Gold-Size for Burnish-Gilding.—Grind fine sal-ammoniac well with a muller and stone ; scrape into it a little beef suet, and grind all wet together ; after which, mix in with a pallet-knife a small proportion of parchment-size with a double proportion of water. When about to use, add parchment-size until it will just flow from the brush.

Another.—Grind a lump of tobacco-pipe clay into a very stiff paste with thin size ; add a small quantity of ruddle and fine black lead, ground very fine, and temper the whole with a small piece of tallow. When ready to use, reduce with parchment size until it will just flow from the brush.

Another.—Grind separately in water, 1 lb. Armenian bole, 2 ozs. red lead, a sufficient quantity of black lead ; mix, and re-grind with a small quantity of olive oil. Reduce with parchment size to the proper consistency.

To Prevent Gold Adhering.—Either one of the following methods will prevent gold-leaf or bronze from adhering to the surface beyond the outlines of the sizing laid on to receive it :

1. Whiting used dry, and applied by means of a pounce bag.

2. Whiting mixed in water, and applied with a soft brush. When the water has evaporated, dust off the superfluous whiting with an ordinary paint duster. By this method a very thin coating of whiting remains, which is free from any grittiness. One advantage gained by the use of whiting thus applied is, it furnishes a whitish ground over which clear varnish or oil-size may be distinctly seen as the striping progresses. After the leaf or bronze has been applied, the work must be carefully washed, so as to insure the removal of the whiting.

3. White of egg reduced with water, and applied with a piece of sponge.

4. A thin wash of starch water, either brushed on with a flat camel-hair brush, or applied with a soft sponge.

5. Take ball liquorice and water, a weak solution, and apply with a soft brush. This may be kept in a bottle ready for use at any time.

6. Cut a new potato in two, amd rub over the part to be sized with the raw face exposed, allowing the juice to remain until dry.

It will be observed that any substance which interposes a film over the varnish, itself being free from tackiness and readily removed by water, will answer the purpose.

Oil Gilding.—Applying the Gold.—If the wood to be gilded is finished with varnish or otherwise, no additional foundation is necessary upon which to lay the gold-leaf ; if the wood is not finished, after it has been smoothed and dusted, give it one or two coats of parchment size, after it is perfectly dry and hard, again smoothing the surface with fine sand-paper. That the gold may not adhere to any part of the work except where the size is hard, powder the surface lightly with whiting from a pounce-bag, which is a small bag made of material sufficiently loose to permit the powdered whiting to sift through as fine dust ; if preferred, any of the preceding receipts for that purpose can be used instead. Remove the surplus whiting with the dusting-brush, and the work is then ready for the size. Apply this with a sable or fit brush of the proper size, carefully observing to make the outer lines of the design clear and sharp, that the work may not appear ragged. Let the size remain until it feels tacky, when the gold may be applied. This is the most difficult part of the operation, and experience is necessary before gold-leaf can be laid smoothly without a wrinkle or a break. Turn a leaf of gold out of the book upon the cushion ; breathe gently upon the centre of the leaf and it will lay flat on the cushion ; cut it to the proper size by bringing the knife perpendicularly over it, and sawing it gently until divided. Take your tip (a brush used for the purpose) and after drawing it lightly over your hair to remove any particles or dust that may be upon it, breathe upon it gently, which will dampen it sufficiently to cause the leaf of gold to adhere to it ; lay the tip upon the leaf of gold and carefully transfer it to the work ; blow upon it gently and it will straighten out and adhere. It may be rendered quite smooth by slightly dabbing it with a bit of cotton. In about an hour wash off the superfluous gold from the edges, with a sponge and water. If the article is to be exposed to the weather or much wear, the gilding may be varnished with copal varnish.

. **Burnish-Gilding.**—As previously stated, this process requires a specially prepared foundation upon which to lay the gold, and as the preparation of this foundation is a distinct trade, the furniture dealer or cabinet-maker seldom finds it necessary to undertake it, the articles coming to his hand ready-prepared for gilding ; but as in repairing picture-frames, cornices, mirror frames, etc., it frequently becomes necessary to renew the foundation, a comprehensive description of the whole process is given.

Preparing the Wood-work.—After smoothing and dusting the work, coat the frames in every part with boiling-hot parchment-size, as previously described, then mix a sufficient quantity of whiting with size to the consistency of thick cream, and with it by means of a brush, coat every part of the frame several times, permitting each coat to become perfectly dry before proceeding with the next. The wood will thus be covered with a layer of hard whiting nearly or quite a sixteenth of an inch in thickness. The size must not be too thick, and when mixed with the whiting should not be so hot as the preliminary coat of size.

Polishing.—When the preparations are quite dry, clean and polish them. To do this, wet a small piece at a time, and, with a smooth, fine piece of cloth, dipped in water, rub the part till all the bumps and inequalities are removed ; and for those parts where the fingers will not enter, as the mouldings, etc., wind the wet cloth round a piece of wood, and by this means make the surface all smooth and even alike.

Where there is carved work, etc., it will sometimes be necessary to bring the mouldings to their original sharpness by means of chisels, gouges, etc., as the preparation will be apt to fill up all the finer parts of the work, which must be thus restored. It is sometimes the practice, after polishing, to go over the work once with fine yellow or Roman ochre ; but this is rarely necessary.

Applying the Size.—Select the proper gold size from the receipts previously given ; add parchment size until it will just flow from the brush ; make it quite hot, and apply it to the wood with a very soft brush, taking care not to make the first coat too thick ; let it dry and give two or three successive coats, after the last brushing it with a stiff brush to remove any inequalities. The work is then ready for the gold.

Laying the gold. The manipulation of the gold leaf has been described under the heading OIL GILDING. In the paint now being described, size used (being water-size, which previously explained is permitted to become hard and dry after being applied) must be moistened to cause the gold-leaf to adhere to it. For this purpose, with a long-haired camel-hair pencil, dipped in water, go over as much of the work as you intend the piece of gold to cover; then lay the gold upon it in the manner previously explained. Be sure that the part to which the gold is applied is sufficiently wet ; indeed it must be floating, or the gold will be apt to crack. Proceed in this manner a little at a time, and do not attempt to cover too much at once, until by experience you are going to handle the gold with freedom.

Burnishing.—When the work is covered with gold, set it by to dry ; there is a particular state or degree of dryness, known only by experience in which the moulding is in a fit state for burishing ; it will probably be ready to burnish in about eight or ten hours, but it will depend on the warmth of the room or state of the air.

When it is ready, those parts intended to be burnished must be dusted with a soft brush ; then wiping the burnisher with a piece of soft wash-leather (quite dry) begin to burnish about an inch or two in length at a time, taking care not to bear too hard, but with a gentle and quick motion, applying the tool until all the parts of the surface are equally bright.

Matting or Dead Gold.—Certain portions only of the work are burnished, according to the fancy, and the facility with which the burnishing tool can be applied ; the remaining parts are now to be deprived of their metallic lustre, to make a more effective contrast with the burnishing. The parts thus treated are said to be matted or dead-gold. The process is as follows :

Grind some vermillion or yellow ochre very fine, and mix a very small portion either with the parchment size or with the white of an egg, and with a very soft brush lay it evenly on the parts to be dulled ; if well done, it will add greatly to the beauty of the work.   Previous to matting, the work must be well cleared of superfluous gold, by means of a soft brush.

Finishing.—In elaborate works it is frequently impossible to lay gold-leaf into all the intricacies of an elaborate design, and the parts thus left bare must be finished by touching up with a small brush charged with shell-gold, or gold-powder, mixed with gum-Arabic to the proper consistency.   The following receipt describes the preparation of shell-gold :

Shelled Gold.—Take any quantity of leaf-gold and grind it with a small portion of honey, to a fine powder, add a little gum-Arabic and sugar-candy, with a little water, and mix it well together ; let it dry.

Silver Size.—Grind pipe-clay fine with a little black-lead and good soap, and add parchment-size as directed for gold-size.

Composition for Frame Ornaments.—The ornaments for gilded mirror-frames, etc., are usually moulded from some plastic substance that is somewhat tougher and more durable than the ordinary gilding foundation of whiting and size.   The proper moulds being prepared they are thoroughly rubbed upon the inside with sweet oil, aud the composition firmly pressed in ; after removing the mould the cast may be dried by a gentle heat, or while still plastic it can be applied in its proper place and bent into any position.   Following are receipts for composition :

Dissolve 1 lb. of glue in 1 gallon of water.   In another kettle boil together 2 lbs. of resin, 1 gill of Venice turpentine, and 1 pint of linseed oil ; mix altogether in one kettle, and boil and stir till the water has evaporated.   Turn the whole into a tub of finely-rolled whiting, and work till it is the consistency of dough.

Boil 7 lbs. of best glue in 7 half-pints of water.   Melt 3 lbs. of white resin in 3 pints of raw linseed oil.   When the above has been well-boiled put them into a large vessel and simmer them for half an hour, stirring the mixture and taking care that it does not boil over.   The whole must then be turned into a box of whiting rolled and sifted, and mixed till it is of the consistency of dough.

To Manipulate Gold Leaf.—Get a piece of paper, thin enough to show shadow of gold-leaf through, slightly wax it, lay it on gold-leaf, the latter will then adhere, and can be easily worked and will come off clean. The paper should be slightly larger than the gold-leaf, and the fingers passed over the paper to make the gold-leaf adhere.

Bronzing.—This is a process for imitating on metal, plaster wood, or other material, the peculiar appearance produced by chemical action upon the surface of bronze metal. It is accomplished by spreading over the surface of the material to be ornamented a very thin coating of bronze-powder, which is caused to adhere either by applying it directly upon a coating of any of the sizes mentioned in the foregoing pages, or by mixing with a vehicle, such as gum-Arabic or transparent varnish. The latter is most desirable, as in the other case, being subject to the direct action of the atmosphere, the bronze-powder soon tarnishes. In ornamenting furniture, bronzing is generally employed to represent gilding, a variety of bronze called gold-bronze being used, which affords an excellent imitation but is not very lasting. It is usually applied after the completion of the other finishing processes, the ground-work being prepared in the manner described under OIL-GILDING, and the size likewise applied as there described. A small wad of cotton batting is then dipped in the bronze and passed gently over the sized portions, causing the bronze to adhere. In the other method—that of applying the bronze by means of a vehicle—the preliminaries of whiting the ground and sizing are not necessary, a small quantity of bronze being simply mixed with the vehicle employed to such a degree of fluidity that it will flow easily, and in that condition applied with a fine brush. Many preparations are used as vehicles such as transparent varnish thinned with turpentine, gum-Arabic, dissolved in water, and gold-size reduced with parchment-size. There are a variety of colors in bronze-powders, and to produce the best effect the size or vehicle should be of a color similar to that of the bronze used ; in gold-size the coloring pigment is ochre, and in its place, for green-bronze, or blue-bronze, may be employed respectively verditer, vermillion or Prussian blue, a very small quantity being sufficient. In bronzing on painted work the ground should be as nearly as possible the color of the bronze to be applied.

THE END.

INDEX.

---

(93)